Marianna Alcoforad

The Letters of a Portuguese Nun

(Marianna Alcoforado)

Marianna Alcoforad

The Letters of a Portuguese Nun
(Marianna Alcoforado)

ISBN/EAN: 9783337016470

Printed in Europe, USA, Canada, Australia, Japan

Cover: Foto ©ninafisch / pixelio.de

More available books at **www.hansebooks.com**

THE LETTERS OF A
PORTUGUESE NUN
(MARIANNA ALCOFORADO)

TRANSLATED BY

EDGAR PRESTAGE

BALLIOL COLLEGE

OXFORD

LONDON

Published by DAVID NUTT

in the Strand

1893

Edinburgh: T. and A. CONSTABLE
Printers to Her Majesty

TO THE AUTHOR OF

'PORTUGAL CONTEMPORANEO'

J. P. DE OLIVEIRA MARTINS

I DEDICATE

THIS BOOK

ERRATA

Page 33, line 12, *read* Guilleragues *for* Guilleraque.
,, 37, ,, 1 (heading), *read* Meu *for* Men.
,, 47, ,, 16, *read* appearances *for* proofs.
,, 49, ,, 6, *read* this beginning *for* this, beginning.
,, 54, ,, 20, *omit* ought to.
,, 57, ,, 18, *read* pauſed *for* paſſed.
,, 62, ,, 8, *insert* one *after* ſome.
,, 63, ,, 9, *read* at times I do not dare to think I could be jealous and yet not diſpleaſe you.
,, 69, ,, 20, *read* your departure baſed on ſuch cruel pretexts.
,, 70, ,, 6, *read* I could never have been on my guard againſt all my weakneſſes.
,, 71, ,, 16, *read* Can it be that you did not care to enjoy them?
,, 74, ,, 11, *read* Methinks, even, I am not at all content.
,, 77, ,, 3, *read* Would it not be very cruel indeed of you to make.
,, 82, ,, 3, *read* What! is all my deſire then to be in vain?
,, 93, ,, 12, *read* the attachment you might have had for another woman could have cauſed me.
,, 96, ,, 19, *read* never forgets what firſt awakened it to feelings.
,, 100, ,, 4, *read* who does not make them render an exact.
,, 102, ,, 5, *read* what confuſion, what a falſe ſtep, what depths.

PREFACE

Y *attempt at an English rendering of the Letters is, I think, the first since the days of Bowles' 'Letters from a Portuguese Nun to an Officer in the French Army,' London, 1808.*[1] *But during the two centuries which have elapsed since their*

[1] An American translation was published in 1890. *Vide* Bibliography.

THE LETTERS OF A

PREFACE *first publication quite a small literature has grown up around them, and they have been turned into several European tongues, the French editions alone amounting to more than thirty. If the numerous so-called 'Replies' and 'Imitations' were added to this reckoning the number would be nearly doubled, and this without taking into account the critiques and studies which have appeared about them. I do not propose here to enter into a comparison of the Letters with those of Heloïse, as many writers have done, but shall content myself with referring the curious to the excellent work of Senhor Cordeiro, 'Soror Marianna. A Freira Portugueza,' Lisbon,* 1888; 2nd edition, 1891. *It is from him that I have learnt nearly all that I know about Marianna, and in my Introduction I have made a liberal use of his book, as well as of M. Assé's preface to the edition of the ' Lettres Portuguises avec les Réponses,' Paris,* 1889, *upon which I have based my rendering.*

If my translation should arouse any interest in things Portuguese, and lead others to read and make versions of such masterpieces of the world's literature as the ' Frei Luiz de Sousa' and the ' Folhas

THE LETTERS OF A

PREFACE *Cahidas' of Garrett, or the poems of João de Deus, I should be more than rewarded for any trouble the present work may have cost me. But who can hope to succeed where Burton has apparently failed? The English public—and the critics too—will probably continue to believe that there is nothing worth reading in Portuguese literature with the exception of the Lusiads. Here too there is perhaps a lesson to be learnt from the Germans, especially from such as Storck, Reinhardstoettner, and Michaëlis de Vasconcellos.*

I should like to thank Mr. York Powell of Christ Church

for the kind help which he has given me in the difficult task of translation. My aim has been throughout to keep as close to the French text as possible—seeing that the original Portuguese is lost,—aided by the masterly re-translation of Senhor Cordeiro. L'Estrange's version—'Five Love Letters from a Nun to a Cavalier,' London, 1678,—is somewhat free at times, but it has aided me in the Third Letter. I have followed Cordeiro in his re-arrangement of the order of the Letters, the Second and Fourth changing places.

The historical facts which concern the hero and heroine

LETTERS OF A NUN

PREFACE *of these Letters I have given briefly in the Introduction, and a Bibliography and Appendix will be found at the end of the volume. The text of the first French edition of* 1669 *has been copied in Paris purposely for this work, and will, it is hoped, add much to its interest and value.*

And so I deliver poor Marianna's passionate Epistles to the consideration of those who can appreciate them and feel for her.

And weeping then she made her moan,
'The night comes on that knows not morn,
When I shall cease to be all alone,
To live forgotten and love forlorn.'

EDGAR PRESTAGE.

BOWDON, 1892.

CONTENTS

	PAGE
PREFACE, ...	ix
INTRODUCTION, ...	3
THE LETTERS, ...	37
FRENCH TEXT, ...	111
BIBLIOGRAPHY, ...	169
APPENDIX, ...	175

INTRODUCTION

A

INTRODUCTION

Fuyd los deleytes, pues non da deleite
Perfecto, nin bueno, nin tan poco sano ;
A todos engaña su falsso afeyte,
Sin sentir mata el su gozo vano.
A todos arriedran del bien soberano,
Jamas no aplazen que no den tristeza,
Aforjan cadenas del sotil Volcano,
Con que encarcelan a toda nobleza.
Cancioneiro de Resende.

'N 1663,' says Sainte-Beuve, 'it became the policy of Louis XIV. to help Portugal against Spain, but the succour which he, gave was indirect; subsidies were secretly furnished, the levying of troops was favoured, and a crowd of volunteers hastened there. Between this small army, commanded by Schomberg, and the feeble

THE LETTERS OF A

INTRO-
DUCTION
Spanish troops which disputed the soil with it, there were each summer many marches and counter-marches with but few results, many skirmishes and small fights, and among the latter, perhaps, one victory. Who troubles himself about it now? The curious reader, however, who only looks to his own pleasure, cannot help saying that all this was good, since the "Letters of the Por‑tuguese Nun" grew from it.'

As Sainte-Beuve indicates, the subject of the 'Letters' forms one of the episodes of the war between Spain and Portugal which followed as a consequence of the Restoration of 1640 and the achievement of the latter's independence under the House of Braganza. This war, which lasted for twenty-eight years, until the final peace in 1668, was intermittent, and carried on only at long intervals owing to the state of the two contending parties. Spain had now entered on the period of her decline, and Portugal was in a hardly better condition after her sixty years' captivity and the exhaustion of her forces which had taken place during the reign of Philip IV. Owing, however, to the aid of France, she had been enabled to hold her own up to 1659; but the news of the Peace of the Pyrenees seemed at first to take from her all hope of preserving her hardly won autonomy. Yet in spite of this, Mazarin, while signing the clause which bound France to abandon the Portuguese cause, determined, with his usual duplicity, that this should not prevent him from secretly aiding an ally whom he had found so useful in the past as a thorn in the side of Spain. Hardly, indeed, had the treaty been made than he began to occupy himself in recruiting for the Portuguese service a number of French officers whom the peace had left without employment. Among these the chief was Schomberg, who went to Lisbon in 1660 as commander-in-chief and to reorganise the Portuguese army. It was not, however,

THE LETTERS OF A

INTRO-
DUCTION until 1663 that the hero of the Letters, Noel Bouton, afterwards Marquis of Chamilly and St. Leger, arrived in the country, which he was to leave four years later with the betrayal of a poor nun as his title to fame. For at the time when Schomberg was already there, we see Chamilly (as he is generally called) assisting at the marriage of his brother to Catherine le Comte de Nonant, referred to in the text (Letter II.).

Three years afterwards, finding himself without military employment in France, he came to Portugal, attracted probably, like so many others, by the reputation of the great captain, with whom he had doubtless established friendly relations during the campaign in Flanders (1656-8).

Our hero, if hero he may be called, was the eleventh son of Nicholas Bouton, Lord of Chamilly, Charangeroux, and, later on, St. Leger, properties of modest size in Burgundy. His family was good, but its attachment to the Princes of

PORTUGUESE NUN

INTRODUCTION

Condé during the Fronde had compromised its position and damaged its fortunes. Noel, the future marquis, was born in 1636, and as soon as his age allowed he entered on a military career. He served through the Flanders campaign under Turenne, and in 1658 was made captain, under the name of the Count of Chamilly, in Mazarin's regiment of cavalry. Reaching Portugal at the end of 1663, or the commencement of 1664, he was given the same rank in a regiment commanded by a French officer of note, Briquemault. Although his name is not mentioned in any of the contemporary notices of the war, we know that he was present at the Siege of Valença de Alcantara (June 1664), at the battle of Castello Rodrigo (in the same month and year), at that of Montes Claros (June 1665), and at the principal sieges which occupied the next two years. In 1665, he was promoted to the rank of colonel, and two years later a diploma of Louis XIV., issued, perhaps, at the instance of his brother, the Governor of Dijon, gave Chamilly a similar post in the French army, with the evident intention of enabling him to leave the Portuguese service when he liked, even though the war with Spain should not be ended. This, taken together with the fact that in the document the space for the month is left blank, is extremely significant, and, as will be seen later on, certainly connects itself with the episode of the 'Letters,' even if it does not enter into their actual history.[1] The diploma of Louis XIV., it may be added, is dated 1667, and the sudden departure of Chamilly took place at the end of that year, so that it seems probable that the French captain, fearing future annoyance or even danger to himself from his *liaison*, had determined to secure a safe retreat.

But let us look for a moment at the authoress of the famous 'Portuguese Letters.'

[1] Cordeiro, *op. cit.*, p. 131, 1st ed.

PORTUGUESE NUN

INTRODUCTION

Marianna Alcoforado was born of a good family in the city of Beja and province of Alemtejo in the year 1640. Her father appears to us in the first years of the Restoration as a man in an influential position, well related, and discharging important commissions both administrative and political. He possessed a large agricultural property, which he administered with attention and even zeal, and was a Cavalier of the Order of Christ, besides being intimate with some of the principal men of the time. He had six children, of whom Marianna, according to Cordeiro, was the second. Life in Beja at that time seems to have been sufficiently insecure, owing to the fact that the province of which it was one of the chief cities formed the theatre of the war, and Beja itself was the chief garrison town. Tumults were constantly arising from quarrels between the various parts of the heterogeneous mass which then composed the Portuguese army, and hence increased care would

THE LETTERS OF A

INTRO-
DUCTION

be necessary on the part of Francisco Alcoforado in order that the education of his daughters might be conducted in such a manner as their position demanded. Hence, too, probably, the reason why Marianna and her sister Catherine entered the Convent of the Conception at an earlier age than was usual. Their father, occupied with administrative and military work on the frontier, would be unable to give them the oversight and attention which quieter times would have allowed.

The Convent of the Conception at Beja was founded in 1467 by the parents of King Emanuel the Fortunate, and, favoured successively by royal and private devotion, it had become one of the most important and wealthy institutions of its kind in Portugal. It was situated at the extreme south of the city, near to the ancient walls, and looked on to the gates still called 'of Mertola,' because they are on the side of the city towards Mertola, distant fifty-four kilometres to the south-west on the right bank of the Guadiana. There is still to be seen the remains of the balcony or verandah from which Marianna first caught sight of Chamilly, probably during some military evolutions (cf. Letter II.), and from it a good view may be obtained over the plains of Alemtejo as they stretch away to the south. Curiously enough, the tradition of Marianna and her fatal love has been perpetuated in the convent, in spite of the attempts, natural enough, on the part of monastic chroniclers and such like to hide all traces of it.

In this as in most other convents there were two kinds of cells—the dormitories, divided into cubicles, and rooms forming independent abodes dispersed throughout the edifice. These latter the nuns of the seventeenth century called their 'houses,'—*as suas casas*,—and it was one of these which Marianna possessed. The former were in accordance with the Constitutions, while the latter, though strictly forbidden, nevertheless existed.

INTRO-
DUCTION
These separate abodes were, it is true, often necessitated by the growth of the convent population, and generally appertained to nuns of a better position, while the dormitories served for those who were either poorer or of an inferior rank. Many of these *casas*, too, were built by private individuals who had some connection or other with the particular convent, and there are indications that the father of Marianna had caused some to be erected in that of the Conception.[1]

From the year 1665 to 1667, then, Beja was, as we have said, the centre of the various military movements in which Chamilly took part under the leadership of Schomberg, and there is no doubt that he spent much of his time there. Marianna was twenty-five years old. She had been intrusted to the Cloister when a child,[2] as she herself tells us, and her

[1] Cf. Cordeiro, *op. cit.*, pp. 147-8 and 300, 1st ed.
[2] This was partly owing to the ideas of the time, and partly for reasons already mentioned, and also because her father wished to build up an estate, to be entailed on heirs-male.

PORTUGUESE NUN

renunciation of the world must have been little more than a form. She had probably made her 'profession' too at the age of sixteen, that provided for by the Constitutions, if not at an earlier date. [INTRODUCTION]

The dull routine of her life was suddenly broken in upon by the sight of a man surrounded with all the prestige of military glory—one who was the first to awaken in her a consciousness of her own beauty—the first to tell her that he loved her, one, moreover, who was ready to throw all his greatness, his present and his future, at her feet.

'I was young; I was trustful. I had been shut up in this convent since my childhood. I had only seen people whom I did not care for. I had never heard the praises which you constantly gave me. Methought I owed you the charms and the beauty which you found in me, and which you were the first to make me perceive. I heard you well talked of; every one spoke in your favour. You did all that was necessary to awaken love in me.'[1] Such is her simple confession, and, comments Cordeiro, nothing more natural.

Their first meeting was probably due to the relations which Chamilly, an officer of rank, had entered into with the Alcoforados, one of the chief families in Beja. There are indications, indeed, that Chamilly and Marianna's eldest brother had met, doubtless in the field, for the latter also followed the profession of arms; and this brother, named Balthazar Vaz Alcoforado, is probably the same as the 'brother' referred to in the Letters as the lovers' go-between. It was for his benefit that Marianna's father had striven for years to build up an estate which was to be entailed on his offspring. But in the year 1669, just at the very time of the great sensation caused by the publication of the Letters in Paris, Balthazar abandoned his military career and all his brilliant prospects in the world to enter the priesthood. It is im-

[1] Letter v.

PORTUGUESE NUN

possible not to hazard a guess, although we know nothing for certain on the point, that his motive for so doing was connected in some way with the almost tragic ending of the *liaison* between his sister and the French captain. But to return:—The customs of the time, curiously enough, allowed a greater relative liberty to nuns as regards the visits which might be paid them than to married women,[1] or, as the Bishop of Gram Pará puts it, 'the liberty of the grating was wide in those miserable times.'[2]

We cannot of course be expected to give an account of the progress of this *liaison*, nor do we wish to indulge in romantic hypotheses.

Chamilly was thirty at the time when he first saw Marianna. Brought up as

---

[1] Asse, *op. cit.*, Preface, p. vi. For an account of the somewhat relaxed character of convent discipline at the time *vide* Cordeiro, pp. 156-164, 1st ed.

[2] 'Muita era a liberdade das grades naquelle miseravel tempo.'

INTRO-
DUCTION
he had been to war as a trade, a man of small intelligence and few scruples, the intrigue would be a pleasant diversion, a means *pour passer le temps* which he would otherwise have found dull enough in a Portuguese provincial town after the Paris of 'Le Grand Monarque.' The seduction and desertion of a poor nun must have seemed all so perfectly natural to one brought up in contact with the loose morality of camp life and in the France of Louis XIV.

In June 1667 the authorities of Beja received an answer from the new King, Don Pedro, to the complaint which they had made of 'the oppression which the French cavalry continued to exercise on this people.'[1] Already, on account of similar complaints, Schomberg had been ordered to move his cavalry from the town and district, but he had disobeyed these orders for strategic reasons. Now, we have already seen that it was between

[1] Cordeiro, *op. cit.*, pp. 326-7, 1st ed.

1665 and 1667 that Chamilly carried on his intrigue with Marianna, and it is just in 1667 that the scandal must have attained greater proportions, coinciding with and ending, not in the withdrawal of the French cavalry, but in the sudden retirement of Chamilly to France. But what, it may be asked, was the reason for the King's order, and what could those 'oppressions' have been in an important city where presumably there was a regular and well-appointed police administration? Has it not a relation, asks Cordeiro, with the incident in the 'Letters,' which would both afflict and irritate the influential family of the nun and the good burgesses of Beja? The special situation of the French captain, on the other hand—his interest in not aggravating the scandal, and the peril for the religious herself in the adoption of violent means, would all naturally counsel the withdrawal of Chamilly.[1]

The danger of remaining longer in

[1] Cordeiro, *op. cit.*, pp. 139-40, 1st. ed.

INTRODUCTION Beja was not in the nature of those which the French colonel could confront with his recognised courage. If he were surprised in the convent, if he were denounced as its violator and as the seducer of a nun, the daughter of a well-known family, and one, too, which was on excellent terms with the new sovereign, neither his own position nor the protection of Schomberg would avail him, since both the one and the other began to lose their importance with the approach of peace.¹

However this may be, certain it is that Chamilly's own excuses for departure, referred to in the 'Letters,' were merely empty pretexts, and a reference to the history of the time will show this. If Louis XIV. needed his presence so much for the invasion of Franche Comté, why not, it may be asked, for the important campaign in Flanders in 1667?

He seems to have left Portugal, too, a

¹ Cordeiro, *op. cit.*, p. 182, 1st ed.

PORTUGUESE NUN

little clandestinely, for no notice is to be met with, as in the case of other French officers, of his asking and obtaining leave from the Portuguese Government, and he probably did not even embark in Lisbon. Already, in the beginning of February 1668, we find him with Louis XIV. in Dijon, so that he must have quitted Beja and the seat of war quite at the end of the preceding year.

INTRO-
DUCTION

It is now that the 'Letters' enter into the history of the lives of Marianna and Noel Bouton de Chamilly. As is well known, they were all written after the latter's retirement from Portugal, and probably between the December of 1667 and the June of 1668, and they express better than any remarks which we could make the stages of faith, doubt, and despair through which poor Marianna passed. As a piece of unconscious, though self-made, psychological analysis they are unsurpassed; as a product of the Peninsular heart they are unrivalled. If they are not, as Theophilo Braga calls

INTRO-
DUCTION

THE LETTERS OF A

them, the only beautiful work produced by his countrymen in the seventeenth century, they are, at any rate, by far the most beautiful. To compare them, as regards literary form, with those of Heloïse would be manifestly unfair, the situation of the two women was so different.[1] Think of the Abbess of the Paraclete, mistress of all the learning of the time, and surrounded by things to console her, or at least to divert her attention, and then regard poor Marianna, persecuted by her family, and liable to the tender mercies of the Inquisition, with none of the comforts, none of the consolations of the former. But if the 'Letters' of Heloïse are superior to those of Marianna from the point of view of correctness of expression and style, they are inferior in all else. The nun's are far more natural, and

---

[1] For a good comparison of the Letters of Marianna and Heloïse see an article entitled 'La Eloísa Portuguesa' in the June number of the review *España Moderna*, 1889, written by Emilio Pardo Bazán.

therefore more beautiful, and the very confusion of feelings and ideas which we should expect from one in her position rather adds to their charm. Finally, the moral character of Heloïse as displayed in her epistles cannot certainly be placed beside that of the Portuguese nun with any advantage.

Henceforth, we only meet with the name of Marianna at intervals—once in 1668, again in 1676 and 1709, and lastly in an obituary notice in 1723.

She, at any rate, is not an example of the well-known saying of Cervantes— 'the Portuguese die of love.' It is true that some words at the end of the Fifth Letter seem to suggest suicide, but there is, on the other hand, throughout the whole of these *ultima verba* an expression of energy and of her determination to tread under foot, if she cannot extinguish, the flames of her passion. Marianna came of a vigorous race, and, in spite of the great infirmities of which her obituary speaks, she lived, as we

THE LETTERS OF A

INTRO-
DUCTION

shall see, to the age of fourscore years and three.

She was made Portress, as mentioned in the Letters, at the beginning of 1668, no doubt to distract her mind by giving her some definite occupation and a sense of responsibility. It is, however, significant, as Cordeiro remarks, that we do not find the name of Marianna, a daughter of one of the principal and most influential families in Beja, filling any more elevated post, whereas her younger sister Peregrina Maria appears in the conventual register as both Amanuensis and Abbess. This sister, before professing in the same convent in 1676, made her will, 'being more than twelve years of age,' and there she spoke of the many obligations which she owed Marianna for having brought her up 'from the age of three years.'[1] Her entering the Conception at such an early age is explained by the fact of the death of her mother, which took place at the end

[1] Cordeiro, *op. cit.*, p. 299, 1st ed.

of 1663 or the beginning of 1664. Again, in 1709, Marianna is mentioned as beaten by only ten votes in an election for the office of Abbess by a certain nun of the name of Joanna de Bulhão, of whom nothing is known.

The next time we hear of her is in 1723, the date of her death. The obituary notice speaks for itself and for her life, since the episode which the 'Letters' contain, and needs no comment. 'On the 28th day of the month of July, in the year 1723, died, in this Royal Convent of Our Lady of the Conception, Mother D. Marianna Alcanforada,[1] at the age of eighty-seven years,[2] all of which she spent in the service of God. She was always very regular in the choir and at the confraternities, and withal fulfilled her (other) obligations. She was very

---

[1] This syntactical extension of the sex to the patronymic was general in the seventeenth century. *Vide* Cordeiro, *op. cit.*, p. 91, 1st ed.

[2] This should be 83. Cf. the extract from the Baptismal Register in Cordeiro, p. 285, 1st ed.

THE LETTERS OF A

INTRO-
DUCTION
exemplary, and none had fault to find with her, for she was very kind to all. For thirty years she did rigid penance and suffered great infirmities with much conformity, desiring to have more to suffer. When she knew that her last hour was come, she asked for all the sacraments, which she received in a state of perfect consciousness, giving many thanks to God for having received them. Thus she ended her life with all the signs of predestination, speaking up to the last hour, in proof of which I, D. An^{ia} Sophia Bap^{ta} de Almeida, Amanuensis of the Convent, wrote this, which I signed on the same day, month and year as above.[1]

D. AN^{IA} SOPHIA BAP^{TA} DE ALM^{DA},
Amanuensis.'

No such obscurity as that which hangs over the life of Marianna hides the

[1] This document was found and transcribed by Cordeiro on pp. 328-9 of his oft-referred-to work, 1st ed.

doings of Chamilly after his return to France. Acts like the famous defence of Grave in 1674 against the Prince of Orange, and that of Oudenarde two years later, marked him out for future distinction. But if he knew how to defend towns he no less could attack and take them. He distinguished himself greatly at the sieges of Gand, Condé, Yprés and Heidelberg, and in 1703 received the recompense of his great services, being made a Marshal of France.

M. Asse tells several anecdotes about him, which *seem* to show that he was a generous man as well as a brave soldier.[1] United in 1671 by a *mariage de convenance* to a lady who, according to S. Simon, was far from being gifted with personal beauty, he was always a most exemplary husband. S. Simon, who knew him well, also tells us that Chamilly was 'the best man in the world, the bravest, and the most honourable.' He says, too, that no one after seeing him

[1] *Op. cit.*, Preface, p. xi.

THE LETTERS OF A

INTRO-
DUCTION

or hearing him speak, could understand how he had inspired such an unmeasured love as that revealed in the famous 'Letters.'[1]

How, then, are we to reconcile the Chamilly of the 'Letters' with the man of whom his contemporaries and friends speak so highly? The publication of the Epistles of Marianna was doubtless due to vanity, a fault which we may certainly credit Chamilly with possessing. It was, too, the custom in seventeenth-century France to hand round copies of letters, either received or written, for the admiration of friends, and thus, what now appears to us a brutal and cynical want of confidence, was then the most natural thing in the world.[2] It is not, however, so easy, even if it is possible, to excuse the conduct of the French captain in the betrayal and desertion of poor Marianna. Posterity, as M. Asse says, especially the

[1] *Memoires*, vol. iii. pp. 372-3; Paris, 1873.
[2] Observation of Senhor Cordeiro, *op. cit.*, p. 6, 1st ed.

feminine portion, has condemned him, and there seems to be no reason why we should seek to reverse the verdict.

It was in 1669 that the first edition of what we know as the 'Portuguese Letters' was published by Claude Barbin, the well-known Parisian bookseller. The translation seems to have been made towards the middle of the year preceding, and shortly after the return of Chamilly to France. The Letters were evidently shown by their possessor as one of those trophies, or at least souvenirs, which persons are accustomed to bring back with them from a foreign country.[1] The incognito, however, was complete, and neither the name of their recipient nor that of their translator was inscribed on this *editio princeps*. That of Marianna, indeed, the authoress, was not known until early in this present century, when in 1810 Boissonade discovered her name written in a copy of

---
[1] Observation of M. Asse.

THE LETTERS OF A

INTRO-
DUCTION
the edition of 1669 by a contemporary hand. The veracity of this note has since been placed beyond doubt by the recent researches of Senhor Cordeiro, who has shown the persistence of a tradition in Beja connecting the French captain and the Portuguese nun.

The success of the first edition was rapid and complete. A second by Barbin, and two in foreign countries, one in Amsterdam, the other in Cologne, all in the same year, attest this. The success, indeed, took such proportions, that from the mutual rivalry of authors and publishers there sprung up a new kind of literature, that of 'les Portugaises.' The Five Letters of the nun had followers like most successful romances, and the title of 'Portuguese Letters' became a generic name applying not only to the imitations which amplified subsequent editions, but also to every kind of correspondence where passion was shown *toute nue*.[1]

[1] Asse, *op. cit.*, Preface, pp. xiii, xiv.

PORTUGUESE NUN

INTRODUCTION

'Brancas,' says Mme. de Sévigné, 'has written me a letter so excessively tender as to make up for all his past neglect. He speaks to me from his heart in every line; if I were to reply to him in the same tone, *ce seroit une Portugaise.*'[1]

In the same year, 1669, Barbin issued a 'second part' of the Portuguese Letters, which was counterfeited shortly afterwards at Cologne, as the real ones had been. This was written, we are told in the preface, by a *femme du monde*, and its publication was suggested by the favour with which the letters of the nun had been received.

The publisher counted, as he said, on the difference of style which distinguished these fresh letters from the original ones, to assure a success as great as the first five had obtained.

After the second part came the so-called 'Replies,' all in the same year,

[1] Letter to Mme. de Grignan in vol. ii., page 284, of the edition of *Paris* 1862.

THE LETTERS OF A

INTRO-
DUCTION
and their publisher tells us in the preface that 'he is assured that the gentleman who wrote them has returned to Portugal.' Shortly afterwards appeared the 'New Replies,' but this time they were given for what they were, 'a *jeu d'esprit* for which the example of Aulus Salinus writing replies to the Heroides of Ovid, and, above all, the beauty of the first Portuguese Letters, should serve as an excuse.'[1]

The motive, then, for the production of the second part of the 'Portuguese Letters' as for that of the 'New Replies' is satisfactorily explained, but how about the 'Replies' themselves? Can we not account for them by supposing that it was felt necessary on the part of the friends of Chamilly to attenuate the sympathy expressed on all sides for the unfortunate nun, and the censure which must naturally have followed such a base betrayal? Hence, proceeds Senhor Cordeiro, the author of this suggestion,

[1] Asse, *op. cit.*, Preface, p. xv.

the publication of these Replies, whose capital idea is to show us the seducer of Marianna under a perfectly different aspect and character from that which readers of the Letters would naturally attribute to him. However this may be, it was not long before the name of their hero came to be printed in editions of the Letters, though, curiously enough, it was first divulged in an edition printed abroad—in Cologne—in 1669, a copy of which is to be found in the British Museum, marked 1085 *b.* 5 (2), containing the following :—

'The name of him to whom they (the Letters) were written is the Chevalier de Chamilly, and the name of him who made the translation is Cuilleraque.'[1]

More strange still, the French editions of the Letters preserved a discreet

---

[1] Director for a time of the *Gazette de France*, and a friend of Mme. de Sévigné and Racine. Boileau described him as

'Esprit né pour la cour et maître en l'art de plaire
Guilleragues qui sais et parler et se taire.'

THE LETTERS OF A

INTRO-
DUCTION

silence as to the name of the recipient with the exception of the 1671 edition of the Replies, until the year 1690, when a similar notice to that above referred to as being in the Cologne edition was made public; so that even in Chamilly's lifetime his name was appended to editions of the Letters as their recipient, and as far as we know he never denied the authenticity of the ascription.

The question as to whether the Letters were originally written in French, or whether they are a translation, hardly needs discussion here, for the principal critics, both French and Portuguese— Dorat, Malherbe, Filinto Elysio and Sousa Botelho—have unanimously decided from the text itself that they are a translation, and a bad one. The last-named says :—' A Portuguese, or indeed any one knowing that language, cannot doubt but that the Five Letters of the Nun have been translated almost literally from a Portuguese original. The con-

PORTUGUESE NUN

struction of many of the phrases is such that, if re-translated word for word, they are found to be entirely in harmony with the genius and character of that language.'[1]

But it is just this baldness for which we should all be truly thankful, because we are thus enabled to listen to what Marianna said, and hear how she said it. Had the translation been what the seventeenth century would have called a good one, we should have known M. Guilleraque well enough, it is true, but only seen the nun 'darkly as through a glass.'

As to the present version, the author can only add to what he has already said in the Preface, by confessing that he feels its inadequacy as much as any of his critics will doubtless do. At the same time, however, if its result be to excite competition, and call forth a better one, his labour will not, he thinks, have been in vain.

[1] Quoted by Cordeiro, *op. cit.*, p. 21, 1st ed.

LETTERS

SHE only said, 'My life is dreary,
  He cometh not,' she said;
She said, 'I am aweary, aweary,
  I would that I were dead!'
            Mariana.—TENNYSON.

FIRST LETTER

Men amigo verdadeiro, quem me vos levou tão longe?
. . . Como vós vos foftes, tudo fe tornou trifteza;
nem parece ainda, fenão que eftava efpreitando já
que vos foffeis.
        BERNARDIM RIBEIRO, *Saudades*, cap. i.

DO but think, my love, how much thou wert wanting in fore-fight. Ah! unfortunate, thou wert betrayed, and thou didft betray me with illufive hopes. A paffion on which thou didft reft fo many profpects of pleafure now only caufes thee a deadly defpair, which is like nothing elfe but the

THE LETTERS OF A

FIRST LETTER

cruelty of the abſence which occaſions it. What! muſt this abſence, to which my ſorrow, all ingenious though it be, cannot give a ſad enough name, deprive me for ever of a ſight of thoſe eyes in which I was wont to feê ſo much love, which made me feel ſo full of joy, which took the place of all elſe to me, and which, in a word, were all that I deſired? Mine eyes, alas! have loſt the only light that gave them life, tears alone are left them, and ceaſeleſs weeping is the ſole employment I have given them ſince I learned that you were bent upon a ſeparation ſo unbearable to me that it muſt ſoon bring about my death. But yet it ſeems to me that I cling in ſome ſort to the ſorrows of

PORTUGUESE NUN

which you are the ſole cauſe. I conſecrated my life to you from the moment when I firſt ſaw you, and I feel a certain pleaſure in ſacrificing it to you. I ſend you my ſighs a thouſand times each day, they ſeek you everywhere, and as ſole recompenſe of ſo much disquietude they bring me back a warning too true, alas, of my unhappineſs : an unhappineſs which is cruel enough to prevent me from flattering myſelf with hope, and which is ever calling to me—Ceaſe, ceaſe to wear thyſelf out in vain, ill-fated Marianna, ceaſe looking for a lover whom thou wilt never ſee again, who has croſſed the ſeas to fly from thee, who is now in France in the midſt of pleaſures, who is not

FIRST LETTER

THE LETTERS OF A

FIRST LETTER thinking for one moment on thy sorrows, who would not thank thee for these pangs for which he feels no gratitude. But no, I cannot make up my mind to think so ill of you, and I am too much concerned that you should right yourself. I do not even wish to think that you have forgotten me. Am I not unhappy enough already without torturing myself with false suspicions? And why should I try so hard to forget all the care you took to prove your love for me? I was so enchanted with it all that I should be ungrateful indeed were I not still to love you with the same transports that my passion lent me when I enjoyed the pledges of your love. How

PORTUGUESE NUN

FIRST LETTER

can the memory of moments fo sweet have become so bitter? And, contrary to their nature, must they serve only to tyrannise over my heart? Alas, poor heart! your last letter brought it into a strange state; it endured such strong pangs that it seemed to be trying to tear itself from me to go and seek for you. I was so overcome by all these violent emotions that I was beside myself for more than three hours.[1] It was as though I refused to come back to a life which I feel bound to lose for you since I cannot preserve it for you. In spite of myself, however, I became myself again; I flattered myself with

---

[1] One of those ecstasies so common in conventual annals is here meant.

FIRST LETTER the feeling that I was dying of love, and befides, I was well pleafed at the thought of being no longer obliged to fee my heart torn by grief at your abfence. Ever fince thofe firft fymptoms I have fuffered much from ill-health, but can I ever be well again until I fee you? And yet I am bearing it without a murmur fince it comes from you. What! is this the reward you give me for loving you fo tenderly? But it matters not; I am refolved to adore you all my life and to care for no one elfe, and I tell you that you too will do well to love no other. Could you ever content yourfelf with a love colder than mine? You will perhaps find more beauty elfewhere (yet you

PORTUGUESE NUN

told me once that I was very beautiful), but you will never find ſo much love: and all the reſt is nothing. Do not fill any more of your letters with trifles: and do not write and tell me again to remember you. I cannot forget you, and as little do I forget the hope you gave me that you would come and ſpend ſome time with me. Alas! why are you not willing to paſs your whole life at my ſide? Could I leave this unhappy cloiſter I ſhould not await in Portugal the fulfilment of your promiſes. I ſhould go fearleſſly over the whole world ſeeking you, following you, and loving you. I dare not flatter myſelf that this can be. I do not care to feed a hope

FIRST LETTER

THE LETTERS OF A

<small>FIRST LETTER</small> that would certainly give me some pleasure, while I wish to feel nothing but sorrow. Yet I confess the chance of writing to you which my brother gave me suddenly aroused in me a certain feeling of joy, and checked for a time the despair in which I live. I conjure you to tell me why you set yourself to bewitch me as you did, when you well knew that you would have to forsake me. Why were you so bent on making me unhappy? Why did you not leave me at peace in my cloister? Had I done you any wrong? But I ask your pardon. I am not accusing you. I am not in a state to think on vengeance, and I only blame the harshness of my fate. It seems to me that in

PORTUGUESE NUN

FIRST LETTER

separating us it has done us all the harm that we could fear from it. It will not succeed in separating our hearts,—for love, more powerful than it, has united them for ever. If you take any interest in my lot write to me often. I well deserve your taking some pains to let me know the state of your heart and fortune. Above all, come and see me. Good-bye. I cannot make up my mind to part from this letter. It will fall into your hands: would I might have the same happiness! Ah, how foolish I am! I know so well that this is impossible. Good-bye. I can no more. Good-bye. Love me always and make me suffer still more.

SECOND LETTER[1]

Das triftezas, não fe pôde contar náda ordenada
mente, porque defordenadamente acontefcem ellas.
BERNARDIM RIBEIRO, *Saudades*, cap. i.

YOUR lieutenant has juft told me that a ftorm has forced you to put into port in the Algarve.[2] I am afraid you have fuffered much on the fea, and fo much has this fear abforbed me that I have thought no more on all my troubles. Do you think, perchance,

[1] No. 4 in all editions and tranflations except that of Cordeiro.
[2] A province in the extreme fouth of Portugal.

LETTERS OF A NUN

that your lieutenant takes more interest in what happens to you than I do? If not, why then is he better informed of it? And then, why have you not written to me? I am unlucky indeed if you have found no time for writing since you left, and still more so if you could have written and would not. Your injustice and ingratitude are too great; but I should be in despair if they were to cause you any harm. I had rather you should remain unpunished than that they should avenge me. I withstand all the proofs which ought to persuade me that you do not love me at all, and I feel much more disposed to yield myself blindly to my passion than to the reasons you give me to

SECOND LETTER

SECOND LETTER complain of your neglect. What mortification you would have fpared me, if, in the days when I firft faw you, your conduct had been as cold as it has feemed to me for fome time now! But who would not have been deceived by fuch ardour as you then fhowed, and who would not have thought it fincere? How hard it is to make up one's mind to doubt for any time the fincerity of thofe one loves! I fee clearly that the leaft excufe is good enough for you; and, without your troubling to make it to me, my love for you ferves you fo faithfully that I cannot confent to find you guilty, except for the fake of enjoying the infinite pleafure of declaring you guiltlefs myfelf. You overcame me by your affiduities, you kindled my paffions with your tranfports, your tendernefs fafcinated me, your vows perfuaded me, but it was the violence of my own love which led me away; and this, beginning at once fo fweet and fo happy, has left nothing behind it but tears, fighs, and a wretched death, without the poffibility of my miniftering any relief to myfelf. It is true that in loving you I enjoyed a pleafure unthought of before, but this very pleafure is now cofting me a forrow, which once I knew nothing of. All the emotions which you caufe me run to extremes. If I had fhown obftinacy in refifting your love, if I had given you any motive for anger or jealoufy in order to draw you on

SECOND LETTER

THE LETTERS OF A

SECOND LETTER the more, if you had detected any artifice in my conduct, if, in a word, I had wiſhed to oppoſe my reaſon to the natural inclination I felt for you, and which you ſoon made me perceive (though doubtleſs my efforts would have been uſeleſs), you might then have puniſhed me ſeverely and uſed your power over me with ſome ſhow of juſtice. But you ſeemed to me worthy of my love before you had told me that you loved me : you gave evidence of a great paſſion for me : I was overjoyed at it, and I gave myſelf up to love you to diſtraction. You were not blinded as I was. Why then did you let me fall into the ſtate in which I now am? What did you want with all my raptures,

SECOND LETTER

which must have been very troublesome to you? You well knew that you would not stay in Portugal for ever. Then why did you single me out to make me so unhappy? Doubtless you might, in this country, have found some woman more beautiful than I am, one with whom you could have enjoyed as much pleasure, —since in this you only sought the grosser kind,—one who would have loved you faithfully as long as you were with her, whom time would have consoled for your absence, and whom you might have left without either treachery or cruelty. You act more like a tyrant bent on persecution than a lover whose only thought should be how to please. Alas! why do

THE LETTERS OF A

SECOND LETTER

you treat fo harſhly a heart which is yours? I can fee very well that you let yourſelf be turned againſt me as eaſily as I let myſelf be convinced in your favour. Without needing to call on all my love, and without imagining that I had done anything out of the way, I ſhould have reſiſted much ſtronger arguments than thoſe can be which have moved you to leave me. They would have feemed to me very weak, and none could have been ſtrong enough to tear me from your ſide. But you were ready to make uſe of the firſt pretexts that you found in order to get back to France. A veſſel was ſailing. Why did you not let it ſail? Your family had written to you. Surely

PORTUGUESE NUN

you know all the perfecutions which I have fuffered from mine? Your honour obliged you to abandon me. Did I take any care of mine? You were forced to go and ferve your king. If all they fay of him is true he has no need of your help, and would have excufed you. I fhould have been only too happy if we could have paffed our whole lives together, but fince it was fated that a cruel abfence fhould feparate us, I think I ought to be glad indeed at the thought of not having been faithlefs, and I would not wifh to have committed fuch a bafe act for anything in the world. What! you who have known the depths of my heart and affection, could you make up your mind to leave me for ever

SECOND LETTER

SECOND LETTER

and expofe me to the dread of feeling that you only remember me in order to facrifice me to fome new paffion?

I well know that I love you as one diftracted. Withal I do not complain of all the violence of my heart's emotions; I am accuftoming myfelf to its tortures, and I could not live without the pleafure which I find and enjoy in loving you in the midft of a thoufand forrows. But a difguft and hatred for everything torments me conftantly; I feel my family, my friends, and this convent unbearable. All I am forced to fee and everything I am obliged to do is hateful to me. I have grown fo jealous of my paffion that methinks all my actions and all my duties ought to have regard to you. Yes,

PORTUGUESE NUN

I have ſcruples in not employing every moment of my life for you. Ah! what ſhould I do without the extremities of hate and love which fill my heart? Could I ſurvive that which inceſſantly fills my thoughts, and lead a quiet cold life? Such a void, and ſuch a lack of feeling, could never ſuit me. All have noticed how completely I am changed in my humour, my manners, and my perſon. My mother[1] ſpoke to me about it, ſharply at firſt, but afterwards more kindly. I know not what I ſaid in reply. I think I confeſſed all to her. Even the ſtricteſt religious pity my condition, and are moved by a certain conſideration and regard for me. Every

SECOND LETTER

[1] The Mother Superior of the convent.

THE LETTERS OF A

SECOND LETTER
one, in fact, is touched by my love: and you alone remain profoundly indifferent. You write me letters at once cold and full of repetitions; the paper is not half filled, and you make it quite clear that you are dying to finiſh them.

Dona Brites has been importuning me for ſeveral days to get me to leave my room, and thinking to divert me ſhe took me for a walk upon the balcony, from which one ſees the gates of Mertola.¹ I went with her, but at once cruel memories aſſailed me, and theſe made me weep for the reſt of the day. She brought me back to my room, and there I

¹ Gates in the city of Beja: ſo called becauſe they are on the ſide which looks toward Mertola, 54 kilometres diſtant. Both Beja and Mertola are in the province of the Alemtejo.

SECOND LETTER

threw myself on the bed and thought a thousand times on the little hope I have of ever being well again. What is done to alleviate only embitters my grief, and I find in the very remedies themselves particular reasons for fresh sorrows. It was from that spot that I often saw you pass by with that air which charmed me so, and I was up on that balcony on the fatal day when I began to feel the first effects of my unhappy passion. Methought you were wishing to please me, although as yet you did not know me. I persuaded myself that you singled me out among all my companions. When you passed I thought you were pleased for me to see you better and admire your skill

SECOND LETTER and grace whilſt you caracoled your horſe. A ſudden fright came over me when you made it go over ſome difficult place. In a word, I intereſted myſelf ſecretly in every act of yours. I felt quite ſure you were not indifferent to me, and I took as meant for me all that you did. You know too well what came of all this; and although I have nothing to hide, I ought not to write to you ſo much about it, leſt I make you more guilty than you are already, if that be poſſible, and leſt I have to reproach myſelf with ſo many uſeleſs efforts to oblige you to be faithful. This you will never be. Can I ever hope that my letters and reproaches will have an effect on your ingratitude that my love

PORTUGUESE NUN

for you and your defertion of me have not had? I know my fad fate too well: your injuftice leaves me not the flighteft reafon to doubt of it, and I am bound to fear the worft, fince you have caft me off. Have you a charm only for me, and do not other eyes find you pleafing? I fhould not be annoyed, I think, were the feelings of others in fome fort to juftify mine, and I would wifh all the women in France to find you agreeable, but none to love you, none pleafe you. This idea is ridiculous and impoffible I well know. I have already, however, found by experience that you are incapable of a great affection, and that you could eafily forget me without any help, and without a

SECOND LETTER

THE LETTERS OF A

SECOND LETTER

fresh love obliging you to it. I would, perhaps, wish you to have some reasonable pretext for your desertion of me. It is true that I should then be more unhappy, but you would not be so guilty. You mean to stay in France, I perceive, without great enjoyments, may be, but in the possession of full liberty. The fatigue of a long voyage, some punctilios of good manners, and the fear of not being able to correspond to my ardent passion, keep you there. Oh do not be afraid of me; I will be content with seeing you from time to time, and knowing only that we are in the same country; but perhaps I flatter myself, and may be you will be more touched by the rigour and hardness of another woman than you have been by all my favours. Can it be that cruelty will inflame you more?

SECOND LETTER

But before engaging yourself in any great paffion, think well on the excefs of my forrows, on the uncertainty of my purpofes, on the contradictions in my emotions, on the extravagance of my letters, on my truftfulnefs, my defpair, my defires, and my jealoufy. Oh! you are on the way to make yourfelf unhappy. I conjure you to profit by my example, that at leaft what I am fuffering for you may not be ufelefs to you. Five or fix months ago you told me a fecret which troubled me, and acknowledged, only too frankly, that you had once loved a lady in your own country. If it

THE LETTERS OF A

SECOND LETTER is she who prevents you from returning here, do not scruple to tell me, that I may fret no more. I am borne up by some remnants of hope still, but I should be well pleased, if it can have no good result, to lose it at a blow, and myself with it. Send me her likeness and some of her letters, and write me all she says. Perchance I shall find reasons wherewith to console myself, or it may be to afflict myself still more. I cannot remain any longer in my present state, and any change whatsoever must be to my advantage. I should also like to have the portrait of your brother and of your sister-in-law.[1] All that concerns

---

[1] Hérard Bouton and Catherine Lecomte de Nonant.

you is very dear to me, and I am wholly given up to what touches you in any way : I have no inclination of my own left. Sometimes, methinks, I could even submit to wait upon her whom you love. Your bad treatment and disdain have broken me down so far that at times I do not dare to think of being jealous of you for fear of displeasing you, and I go so far as to think that I should be doing the greatest wrong in the world were I to upbraid you. I am often convinced that I ought not to let you see, so madly as I do, feelings which you disown. An officer has now been waiting long for this letter. I had resolved to write it in such a way that you might re-

SECOND LETTER

SECOND LETTER ceive it without annoyance, but as it is, it is too extravagant, and I muſt cloſe it. Alas! I cannot bring myſelf to this. I ſeem to be ſpeaking to you whilſt I write, and you ſeem to be more preſent to me. The next[1] letter ſhall neither be ſo long nor ſo troubleſome; you may open and read it aſſured of this. It is true that I ought not to ſpeak of a paſſion which diſpleaſes you, and I will not ſpeak of it again. In a few days it will be a year ſince I gave myſelf up to you without reſerve. Your love ſeemed to me very warm and ſincere, and I ſhould never have thought that my favours would ſo annoy you as to oblige

[1] Both Cordeiro and the French texts read 'firſt,' which does not make ſenſe.

you to voyage five hundred leagues and expofe yourfelf to the rifk of fhipwreck to efcape from them. I have not deferved fuch treatment as this at any man's hands. You may remember my modefty, my fhame, and my confufion, but you do not remember what would make you love me in fpite of yourfelf. The officer who is to carry you this letter fends to me for the fourth time to fay that he wifhes to be gone. How prefsing he is! doubtlefs he is leaving fome unhappy lady in this country.

Good-bye. It cofts me more to finifh this letter than it coft you to quit me, perhaps for ever. Goodbye. I do not dare give you a

SECOND LETTER

thoufand names of love, nor abandon myfelf to all my feelings without reftraint. I love you a thoufand times more than my life, and a thoufand times more than I think for. How dear you are to me, and yet how cruel! You do not write to me. I could not help faying this to you again. But I am beginning afrefh, and the officer will be gone. What matters it? Let him go. 'Tis not fo much for your fake that I write as for my own. I only feek fome folace. Befides, the very length of my letter will frighten you, and you will not read it. What have I done to be fo unhappy? And why have you poifoned my life? Why was I not born in fome other country? Good-

PORTUGUESE NUN

bye, and forgive me. I dare not now pray you to love me. See to what my fate has brought me. Good-bye!

SECOND LETTER

THIRD LETTER

... Que efte pequeno penhor de meus longos fufpiros vá ante os feus olhos. Muitas outras coufas defejo, mas efta me feria affaz.'—BERNARDIM RIBEIRO, *Saudades*, cap. i.

WHAT will become of me, and what would you have me do? How far I am now from all that I had looked forward to! I hoped that you would write me from every place you paffed through, and that your letters would be very long ones,—that

LETTERS OF A NUN

you would feed my love by the hope of seeing you again, that full trust in your fidelity would give me some sort of rest, and that I should then remain in a state bearable enough, and without the extremes of sorrow. I had even thought of some poor plans of endeavouring, as far as possible, my own cure, in case I could but once assure myself that you had entirely forgotten me. The distance which you are at, certain impulses of devotion, the fear of entirely destroying the remainder of my health by so many wakeful nights and so many cares, the improbability of your return, the coldness of your love, and your last good-byes, your unkind pretexts

THIRD LETTER

THIRD LETTER for departure, and a thousand other reasons which are only too good and too useless, seemed to offer me a safe refuge if I needed one. Having indeed only myself to reckon with, I was never able to imagine myself so weak, nor foresee all that I now suffer. Ah! how pitiful it is for me,—I that am not able to share with you my sorrows, and must be all alone in my grief! This thought is killing me, and I almost die of horror when I think that you were never really affected by all the bliss that we shared. Yes, I understand now the untruth of all your transports. You betrayed me every time you told me that your supreme delight was to be alone with me. It is to my

PORTUGUESE NUN

importunities alone that I owe your warmth and paſſion. Deliberately and in cold blood you formed a deſign to kindle my love; you only regarded my paſſion as your triumph, and your heart was never deeply touched. Are you not very wretched? and have you ſo little delicacy that you made no other uſe of my love but this?

How then can it be that with ſuch love I have not been able to make you entirely happy? It is ſolely for love of you that I regret the infinite pleaſures you have loſt. Why would you not enjoy them? Ah! if you only knew them you would doubtleſs find them much greater than that of having deceived me, and you would have experienced

THIRD LETTER

THE LETTERS OF A

THIRD LETTER

how much happier it is, and how much more poignant it is to love violently than to be loved. I know not what I am, or what I do, or what I wish for. I am torn asunder by a thousand contrary emotions. Can a more deplorable state be imagined? I love you to distraction, and therefore I spare you sufficiently not to dare to wish that the same emotions should trouble you. I should kill myself or die of grief without were I to be assured that you were never having any rest, that your life was as anxious and disturbed as mine, that you were weeping ceaselessly, and that everything was hateful to you. I cannot bear my own sufferings, how then could I support the sor-

PORTUGUESE NUN

row a thousand times more grievous which yours would give me? I cannot, on the other hand, make up my mind to wish that you should think no more of me; and to speak frankly, I am furiously jealous of all that gives you pleasure, and comes near to your heart and fancy in France. I know not why I write to you. I perceive that you will only pity me, and I wish for none of your pity. I hate myself when I look back on all that I have sacrificed for you. I have lost my honour. I have exposed myself to the anger of my parents, to all the severity of the laws of this country against religious, and finally to your ingratitude, which has seemed to me the greatest of all my evils.

THIRD LETTER

THE LETTERS OF A

THIRD LETTER Withal, I feel that my remorſe is not real, and that I would willingly, with all my heart, have run the greateſt riſks for the love of you, and that I experience a ſad pleaſure in having riſked my life and honour in your ſervice. Ought not all that I hold moſt dear to be at your diſposal? Ought I not to be ſatisfied at having employed it as I have done? Methinks I am ſcarcely content with my ſorrows, or the exceſs of my love, although I cannot, alas! flatter myſelf ſufficiently to be content with you. I live, unfaithful that I am; I do as much to preſerve my life as to loſe it. Ah! I am dying of ſhame. Is my deſpair then only in my letters? If I loved you, as I have told you a thousand times, should I not have been dead long ago? I have deceived you, and you may rightly complain of me. Alas! why do you not complain of me? I saw you leave, I can never hope to see you come back, and in spite of all I yet breathe! I have deluded you. I ask your pardon, but do not grant it me. Treat me harshly —say my love for you is too weak; be more hard to please; tell me that you would have me die of love for your sake. Help me thus, I conjure you, to overcome the weakness of my sex, and to put an end to all my wavering in real despair. Doubtless a tragic end would force you to think of me often, my memory would become dear to you,

THE LETTERS OF A

THIRD LETTER

and perhaps you would be really touched by ſo uncommon a death. Would not death be better than the ſtate to which you have brought me? Good-bye. How I wiſh that I had never ſeen you. Ah! I feel how falſe this phraſe is, and I know at the very moment in which I write it that I had far rather be unhappy in my love for you than never have ſeen you. Willingly, and without a murmur, I conſent to my evil fate, ſince it has not been your wiſh to make it happier. Good-bye; promiſe me a few tender regrets if I die of grief, or at leaſt that you will let the violence of my love give you a diſguſt and repulſion for everything elſe. This conſolation will ſuffice me, and if

PORTUGUESE NUN

I muſt leave you for ever, I would wiſh not to leave you to another woman. You ſurely would not be ſo cruel as to make uſe of my deſpair to render yourſelf more agreeable, and to let it be ſeen that you have inſpired the greateſt paſſion in the world? Good-bye once again. My letters are too long, and I do not regard you ſufficiently. I ask your pardon, and dare hope that you will ſhow ſome indulgence to a poor mad woman who was not ſo, as you know, before ſhe loved you. Good-bye. Methinks I too often ſpeak to you of the inſufferable ſtate in which I am, yet I thank you from the bottom of my heart for the deſpair which you cauſe me, and

THIRD LETTER

LETTERS OF A NUN

THIRD LETTER   I hate the peace which I lived in before I knew you.

Good-bye! My love grows ſtronger each moment. Oh what a world of things I have to tell you of!.

FOURTH LETTER[1]

> Ai goftos fugitivos!
> Ai gloria já acabada e confumida!
> Ai males tão efquivos!
> Qual me deixais a vida!
> Quão cheia de pezar! quão deftruida!
> CAMÕES, *Ode* iii.

METHINKS I do the greateft poffible wrong to the feelings of my heart in trying to make them known to you in writing. How happy fhould I be could you judge of my paffion by the violence of

[1] No. 2 in all editions and tranflations except that of Cordeiro.

FOURTH LETTER yours! But I muſt not compare my feelings with yours, though I cannot help telling you, much leſs ſtrongly than I feel it, it is true, that you ought not to maltreat me as you do by a forgetfulneſs which thruſts me into deſpair, and which even for you is diſhonourable. It is but fair that you ſhould allow me to complain of the evils which I clearly foreſaw when I perceived that you were reſolved to forſake me. I well know now that I deluded myſelf, thinking as I did that you would deal with me in better faith than is uſually the caſe, becauſe the exceſs of my love put me, it ſeemed, above all kind of ſuſpicion, and merited more fidelity than is ordinarily met with. But your wifh to deceive me overruled the justice you owe me for all that I have done for you. I fhould ftill be unhappy even if you only loved me becaufe I love you, and I would wifh to owe it all to your inclination alone. But fo far is this from being the cafe that I have not received a fingle letter from you for the laft fix months. I put down all my misfortunes to the blindnefs with which I gave myfelf up to love of you. Should I not have forefeen that the end of my pleafure would come before that of my love? Could I expect you to ftay all your life in Portugal and give up both country and career and think only of me? Nothing can lighten my forrow,

THE LETTERS OF A

FOURTH LETTER

and the remembrance of all that I enjoyed fills me with defpair. What! are all my hopes to be utterly futile? and fhall I never see you again in my room with all the ardour and paffion which you once fhowed? But, alas! I am deceiving myfelf, and I know too well that all the feelings that filled my head and heart were only excited in you by a few pleafures, and that they both ended at the fame time. I ought then in thofe moments of fupreme happinefs to have called reafon to my aid to moderate the deadly excefs of my delight, and to foretell to me all that I am now fuffering. But I gave myfelf up to you entirely, and I was not in a ftate to think of anything which would have poisoned my pleasure and prevented me from fully enjoying the pledges of your ardent love. I was too much delighted to feel that I was with you to think that you would one day be far from me. I remember, however, having told you sometimes that you would make me unhappy, but these fears were soon dissipated, and I took pleasure in sacrificing them to you, and in giving myself up to the enchantment and the faithlessness of your protests. I see clearly the remedy for all the evils which I suffer, and I should be soon rid of them if I loved you no more. But alas! what a remedy! I had rather suffer still more than forget you. Does that, alas! depend on me? I

FOURTH LETTER

FOURTH LETTER cannot reproach myſelf with having for a ſingle moment wiſhed to ceaſe to love you. You are more to be pitied than I am, and all my ſufferings are better than the cold pleaſures which your French mistreſſes give you. I do not envy you your indifference, and you make me pity you. I defy you to forget me entirely. I flatter myſelf that I have put you in a ſtate in which you can enjoy but imperfect pleaſures without me, and I am happier than you becauſe I am more occupied. Some little time ago I was made portreſs of this convent. All who ſpeak to me think that I am mad. I know not what I anſwer them. The religious muſt be as mad as myſelf to have

PORTUGUESE NUN

thought me capable of taking care of anything. Oh how I envy the good fortune of Manoel and Francifco![1] Why am I not always with you, as they are? I would have followed you and waited upon you with more goodwill, it is certain. To fee you is all that I defire in this world. At leaft remember me; for you to remember me will content me, but I dare not make fure even of this. I ufed not to limit my hopes to your remembrance of me when I faw you daily, but you have taught me the neceffity of fubmitting to all that you wifh. Withal I do not repent of having adored you; I am glad that you betrayed me, and your abfence,

FOURTH LETTER

[1] Two of Chamilly's fervants.

THE LETTERS OF A

FOURTH LETTER

cruel though it is, and perhaps eternal, diminiſhes in no way the violence of my love. I wiſh everybody to know it; I make no mystery of it; and I pride myſelf on having done for you all that I did againſt every kind of decorum. My honour and religion conſiſt but in loving you to diſtraction all my life through, ſince I have begun to love you. I am not telling you all this to oblige you to write to me. Oh do not force yourſelf; I only wiſh from you what comes ſpontaneouſly, and I reject all the teſtimonies of your love which you can control. I ſhall find pleaſure in excuſing you, becauſe you will perhaps be glad not to have the trouble of writing to me, and I feel deeply disposed to pardon you all your faults. A French officer had the charity to talk to me of you for three hours this morning; he told me that peace was made with France.[1] If this is so could you not come and see me, and take me to France? But I do not deserve it. Do as you please, for my love no longer depends on the way in which you may treat me. I have not been well for a single moment since you left, and my only pleasure has been that of repeating your name a thousand times each day. Some religious who know the deplorable state into which you have plunged me often speak to me of

FOURTH LETTER

---

[1] The treaty of Aix-la-Chapelle, which was signed May 2nd, 1668, ratified this peace and put an end to the war called 'of Devolution.'

FOURTH LETTER you. I leave my room, where you fo often ufed to come to fee me, as little as poffible, and I conftantly look at your likenefs, which is to me a thoufand times dearer than life itfelf. It gives me fome pleafure, but alfo much forrow, when I confider that I fhall perchance never fee you again.

Why muft it be that I fhall poffibly never fee you again? Have you then left me for ever? I am in defpair. Your poor Marianna can no more; fhe is almoft fainting while fhe finifhes this letter. Good-bye, Good-bye. Have pity on me.

FIFTH LETTER

> Eſtou pôſto ſem medo
> A tudo o que o fatal deſtino ordene:
> Póde ſer que canſado,
> Ou ſeja tarde, ou cedo,
> Com pena de penar-me, me deſpene.
> CAMÕES, *Canção* ix.

AM writing to you for the laſt time, and I hope to let you ſee by the difference in the terms and manner of this letter that you have at laſt perſuaded me that you no longer love me, and that therefore I ought no longer to love you. I will ſend you on the

FIFTH LETTER

first opportunity all that I still have of yours. Do not be afraid that I shall write to you; I will not even put your name on the packet. With all these details I have charged Dona Brites,[1] whom I have accustomed to confidences very different from this. Her care will be less suspected than mine. She will take all the necessary precautions, that I may be assured that you have received the portrait and bracelets which you gave me. I wish you to know, however, that for some days I have felt as if I could burn and tear up these tokens of your love, once so dear to me. But I have revealed such weakness to

[1] D. Brites de Noronha was a professed nun and a companion of Marianna in the convent of the Conception at Beja.

PORTUGUESE NUN

FIFTH LETTER

your eyes that you would perhaps never have believed me capable of going to a like extremity. I wish, however, to enjoy all the pain I have experienced in separating from them, and cause you some vexation at least. I confess, to your shame and mine, that I found myself more attached to these trifles than I should like to tell you, and I felt that I had again need of all my reasoning powers to enable me to get rid of each object in spite of my flattering myself that I cared no more for you. But, provided with such good reasons as mine, one always achieves the end one seeks. I have placed them in the hands of Dona Brites. What tears this resolution cost me! After

THE LETTERS OF A

FIFTH LETTER

a thousand different emotions and doubts which you know not of, and of which I shall certainly not give you an account, I have conjured her to speak no more to me of these baubles, and never to give them back to me even though I should beg to see them once again, and, in a word, to send them you without letting me know.

It is only since I have been employing all my efforts to heal myself that I have come to know the excess of my love, and I fear that I should not have dared to take it in hand had I foreseen so many difficulties and such violence. I am persuaded that I should have experienced less disagreeable emotions in loving you, ungrateful though you are, than in quitting you for ever. I have found out that you were lefs dear to me than my paffion; and I have had hard work to fight againft it even after your infulting behaviour made you hateful to me. The pride natural to my fex has not helped me to refolve aught againft you. Alas! I fuffered your fcorn, and I could have fupported your hate and all the jealoufy which your attachment for another woman has given me. I fhould have had at leaft some paffion to combat, but your indifference is infupportable to me. Your impertinent proteftations of friendfhip, and the ridiculous civilities of your laft letter, convince me that you have received all thofe which I have written to

FIFTH LETTER you, that they have ſtirred no emotions in your heart, and yet that you have read them. O ungrateful man! I am ſtill fooliſh enough to be in deſpair at not being able to flatter myſelf that they have not reached you or been given into your hands. I deteſt your frankneſs. Did I ever aſk you to tell me the truth ſincerely? Why did you not leave me my love? You had only not to write; I did not ſeek to be enlightened. Am I not unhappy enough with all my inability to make the taſk of deceiving me difficult to you, and now at not being able to exculpate you. Know that I am convinced that you are unworthy of all my love, and that I underſtand all your baſe qualities.

PORTUGUESE NUN

FIFTH LETTER

If, however, all that I have done for you deserves that you should pay some slight regard to the favours I ask of you, write no more to me, I beg you, and help me to forget you entirely. If you were to show, even slightly, that you had felt some grief at the reading of this letter, perchance I should believe you. Perchance, also, your acknowledgment and assent would vex and anger me, and all that would inflame my love afresh. Do not then take any account of my life, or you would doubtless overthrow all my plans, however you entered into them. I care not to know the result of this letter, and I beg of you not to disturb the peace which I am preparing for myself. Methinks you

FIFTH LETTER may content yourſelf with the harm which you have already cauſed me, whatever be the intention you formed to make me miſerable. Do not tear me from my ſtate of uncertainty; I hope in time to combine with it something like peace of heart. I promiſe not to hate you; indeed I diſtruſt any violent feelings too much to adventure that. I am perſuaded that I ſhould find, it may be in this country, another lover more faithful and handſomer; but, alas! who could make me feel love? Would a paſſion for another man fill my thoughts? Has mine had any power over you? Have I not experienced that a tender heart never forgets him who firſt made it know feelings it knew not that it was capable of? I have found that all the feelings of such a heart are bound up with the idol it has created for itself—that its first impressions, its first wounds, can neither be healed nor effaced — that all the passions which offer their help and attempt to fill and content it promise it but vainly an emotion which it never feels again—that all the pleasures which it seeks, without any desire of finding them, serve only to convince it that nothing is so dear as the remembrance of its sorrows? Why have you made me feel the imperfection and bitterness of an attachment which cannot endure for ever, and all the evils that result from a violent love, when it is not mutual? Why is it that blind

THE LETTERS OF A

FIFTH LETTER inclination and cruel fate agree as a rule in determining us in favour of those who could only love others? Even if I could hope for some diversion in a new engagement, and could find a man of good faith, I pity myself so much that I should have great scruples in putting the worst man in the world in the condition to which you have brought me; and although I may not be obliged to spare you I could not make up my mind to avenge myself so cruelly, even though it were to depend on me, by a change which I certainly do not foresee. At this very moment I am seeking excuses for you, and I understand that a religious is not as a rule loveable. Methinks, however, if reason guided one's choice one ought to be more attached to them than to other women. Nothing prevents their thinking conſtantly of their paſſion, and they are not turned aſide by a thouſand things which divert and occupy the mind in the world. Surely it cannot be very pleaſing to ſee thoſe whom one loves ever diſtracted by a thouſand trifles, and one muſt needs have but little delicacy to ſuffer them (without being in deſpair at it) to talk of nothing but aſſemblies, dreſs, and promenades. One is conſtantly expoſed to freſh jealouſies, for they are tied down to attentions, politeneſſes, and converſations with all. Who can be aſſured that they find no pleaſure in all theſe occaſions, and that they always endure

THE LETTERS OF A

FIFTH LETTER

their hufbands with extreme difguft and never of their freewill? Ah, how they ought to diftruft a lover who does not render them an exact account of all, who believes eafily and without difquiet what they tell him, who in unruffled truft fees them bound to all these fociety duties. But I do not feek to prove to you by good reafons that you ought to love me; thefe are very ill means, and I have made ufe of much better, without fuccefs. Too well do I know my fate to try to rife above it. I fhall be miferable all my life. Was I not fo even when I faw you daily? I was dying for fear that you would not be faithful. I wifhed to fee you every moment, and I could not.

PORTUGUESE NUN

FIFTH LETTER

The danger you ran in entering the convent troubled me. I almoſt died when you were with the army. I was in deſpair at not being more beautiful and more worthy of you. I uſed to murmur againſt my modeſt rank,[1] and I often thought that the attachment you appeared to cheriſh for me would be hurtful to you in ſome way. Methought I did not love you enough. I feared the anger of my parents againſt you, and I was, in a word, in as lamentable a ſtate then as now. If you had ſhown me any ſigns of affection ſince you left Portugal I ſhould have made every effort to leave it, and I would have diſguiſed myſelf

---

[1] Marianna refers to her condition as a Franciſcan nun in a ſmall provincial town, not to the rank of her family, which was as good as that of her lover.

FIFTH LETTER to go and find you. Ah, what would have became of me if you had troubled no more about me after I had arrived in France?—what fcandal, what trouble, what depths of fhame for my family which is fo dear to me fince I have ceafed to love you! I quite underftand, you fee, that I might have been even more wretched than I am. At leaft for once in my life I am speaking reafonably to you. How delighted you will doubtlefs be at my moderation, and how pleafed with me? But I wifh not to know it. I have already prayed you not to write to me again, and I repeat it now. Have you never reflected on the way in which you have treated me? Have you never

FIFTH LETTER

confidered that you owe me more than any one elſe in the world? I have loved you as a mad woman might. How I defpifed everything elſe!

Befides, you have not acted like an honourable man. You muſt have had a natural averfion for me, fince you have not loved me to diſtraction. I allowed myfelf to be enchanted by very mediocre qualities. What have you ever done to pleafe me? What facrifice have you made for me? Did you not always feek a thoufand other pleafures? Did you ever give up gaming or the chafe? Were you not ever the firſt to leave for the army, and did you not always come back the laſt? You expofed your-

THE LETTERS OF A

FIFTH LETTER
ſelf raſhly, although I had begged you to ſpare yourſelf for my ſake. You never ſought the means of ſettling down in Portugal, where you were eſteemed. A ſingle letter from your brother made you leave without a moment's heſitation. Do I not know that during the voyage you were in the beſt of humours? It muſt be confeſſed that I ought to hate you with a deadly hatred. Ah, I have brought down all theſe misfortunes on myſelf. I accuſtomed you from the firſt to a boundleſs love, and that with too much ingenuouſness, while one needs to employ artifice to make one's ſelf loved. One ſhould ſeek the means of ſkilfully exciting it, for love of itſelf does not engender love. You

PORTUGUESE NUN

wished me to love you, and since you had formed this design there is nothing that you would not have done to accomplish it. You would even have made up your mind to love me had that been neceffary, but you knew that you could fucceed in your enterprife without paffion, and that you had no need of it. What treachery! did you think that you could deceive me with impunity? If any chance brings you again to this country, I declare that I will hand you over to the vengeance of my kinsfolk. I have lived too long, in an abandonment and idolatry which ftrikes me with horror, and feelings of remorfe perfecute me with unbearable feverity. I feel a lively fhame for

FIFTH LETTER

<small>FIFTH LETTER</small> the crimes which you have made me commit, and I have no more, alas! the love which prevented me from comprehending their enormity. When will this heart of mine ceafe to be torn? When fhall I be freed from thefe cruel trammels?

In fpite of all, methinks I do not wifh you harm, and could refolve to confent to your being happy. But how could you be so, if you had a true heart? I mean to write you another letter, to fhow you that I fhall perchance be more at peace fome day. What pleafure I fhall find in being able to reproach you for your injuftice when I am no longer fo vividly touched by it, in letting you know that I defpife you, and that I can fpeak with indifference of your deceit, that I have forgotten all my pleasures and all my sorrows, and that I only remember you when I wish to do so! I recognise that you have a great advantage over me, and that you have inspired in me a love which has upset my reason; but at the same time you should take little credit to yourself for it. I was young, I was trustful, I had been shut up in this convent since my childhood,[1] I had only seen people whom I did not care for. I had never heard the praises which you constantly gave me. Methought

FIFTH LETTER

---

[1] Marianna was about twenty-six years of age when she first met Chamilly. She had naturally made her profession at sixteen and had been confided to the care of the convent at twelve, or even much earlier, like her sister.

THE LETTERS OF A

FIFTH LETTER

I owed you the charms and the beauty which you found in me, and which you were the firſt to make me perceive: I heard you well talked of; every one ſpoke in your favour: you did all that was neceſſary to awake love in me. But I have at laſt returned to myſelf from this enchantment. You yourſelf helped me greatly, and I confeſs that I had much need of it. When I return you your letters I ſhall take care to keep the laſt two which you wrote me; and I ſhall re-read them more often than I have the previous ones, in order that I may not relapſe into my former weakneſs. Ah! how dear they coſt me, and how happy I ſhould have been if you had allowed

PORTUGUESE NUN

FIFTH LETTER

me to love you always. I well know that I am ſtill a little too much taken up with my reproaches and your faithleſſneſs, but remember that I have promiſed myſelf a ſtate of greater peace, and that I ſhall reach it, or take ſome deſperate reſolve againſt myſelf, which you will learn, without great diſpleaſure. But I wiſh no more of you, and I am fooliſh to repeat the ſame things ſo often. I muſt leave you, and think no more on you. I even think that I ſhall not write to you again. Am I under any obligation to render you an exact account of all I do?

LETTRES PORTVGAISES
TRADVITES
EN FRANÇOIS

LETTRES
PORTVGAISES
TRADVITES
EN FRANÇOIS

A PARIS,

Chez CLAVDE BARBIN, au
Palais, fur le fecond Perron
de la fainte Chapelle.

M. DC. LXIX
Avec Privilége du Roy

AV LECTEVR

J'AY trouué les moyens auec beaucoup de soin & de peine, de recouurer vne copie correcte de la traduction de cinq Lettres Portugaises, qui ont esté écrites a vn Gentilhomme de qualité, qui seruoit en Portugal. J'ay veu tous ceux qui se connoissent en sentimens, ou les loüer, ou les chercher auec tant d'empressement, que j'ay crû que ie leur ferois vn singulier plaisir de les imprimer. Ie ne sçay point le nom de celuy auquel on les à écrites, ny de celuy qui en a fait la traduction, mais il m'a semblé que ie ne deuois pas leur déplaire en les rendant publiques. Il est difficile quelles n'eussent, enfin, pary auec des fautes d'impression qui les eussent défigurées.

PREMIERE LETTRE

CONSIDERE, mon amour, jusqu'à quel excez tu as manqué de preuoyance. Ah mal-heureux! tu as efté trahy, & tu m'as trahie par des efperances trompeufes. Vne paffion fur laquelle tu auois fait tant de projets de plaifirs, ne te caufe prefentement qu'vn mortel defefpoir, qui ne peut eftre comparé qu'à la cruauté de l'abfence, qui le caufe. Quoy? cette abfence, à laquelle ma douleur, toute ingenieufe qu'elle eft, ne peut donner vn nom affez funefte, me priuera donc pour toujours de regarder ces yeux, dans lefquels je voyois tāt d'amour, & qui me faifoient connoître des mouuemēs, qui me combloient de joye, qui me tenoient lieu de toutes

LETTRES TRADVITES

PREMIERE ETTRE choses, & qui enfin me suffisoient ? Helas ! les miens sont priuez de la seule lumiere, qui les animoit, il ne leur reste que des larmes & je ne les ay employez à aucun vsage, qu'à pleurer sans cesse, depuis que j'appris que vous estiez enfin resolu à vn éloignement, qui m'est si insupportable, qu'il me fera mourir en peu de temps. Cependant il me semble que j'ay quelque attachement pour des malheurs, dont vous estes la seule cause : Ie vous ay destiné ma vie aussi-tost que je vous ay veu ; & je sens quelque plaisir en vous la sacrifiant. I' enuoye mille fois le jour mes soupirs vers vous, ils vous cherchent en tous lieux, & ils ne me rapportent pour toute recompense de tant d'inquietudes, qu'vn aduertissement trop sincere, que me dōne ma mauuaise fortune, qui a la cruauté de ne souffrir pas, que je me flatte, & qui me dit à tous momens ; Cesse, cesse Mariane infortunée de te consumer vainement : & de chercher vn Amant que tu ne verras iamais ; qui a passé les Mers pour te fuir, qui est en France au milieu des plaisirs, qui ne pense pas vn seul moment à tes douleurs, & qui te dispense

de tous ces tranfports, defquels il ne te
fçait aucun gré ? mais non, je ne puis
me refoudre à juger fi injurieufement de
vous, & je fuis trop intereffée à vous
juftifier : Ie ne veux point m'imaginer
que vous m'auez oubliée. Ne fuis-je
pas affez malheureufe fans me tourmen-
ter par de faux foupçons ? Et pourquoy
ferois-je des efforts pour ne me plus
fouuenir de tous les foins, que vous
auez pris de me temoigner de l'amour ?
I'ay efté fi charmée de tous ces foins,
que je ferois bien ingrate, fi je ne vous
aymois auec les mefmes emportemens,
que ma Paffion me donnoit, quand je
joüiffois des témoignages de la voftre.
Comment fe peut-il faire que les fouuenirs
des momens fi agreables, foient deuenus
fi cruels ? & faut-il que contre leur
nature, ils ne feruent qu'à tyrannifer
mon cœur ? Helas ! voftre derniere
lettre le reduifit en vn eftrange état : il
eut des mouuemens fi fenfibles qu' il fit,
ce femble, des efforts, pour fe feparer de
moy, & pour vous aller trouuer : Ie fus fi
accablée de toutes ces émotions violentes,
que je demeuray plus de trois heures
abandonnée de tous mes fens : je me

PREMIERE
LETTRE

LETTRES TRADVITES

PREMIERE LETTRE défendis de reuenir à vne vie que je dois perdre pour vous : puis que je ne puis la cōnferver pour vous, je reuis enfin, malgré moy la lumiere, je me flatois de fentir que je mourois d'amour ; & d'ailleurs j'eftois bien-aife de n'eftre plus expofée à voir mon cœur déchiré par la douleur de voftre abfence. Apres ces accidens, j'ay eu beaucoup de differētes indifpofitions : mais, puis-je jamais eftre fans maux, tant que je ne vous verray pas ? Ie les supporte cependant fans murmurer, puis qu'ils viennent de vous. Quoy ? eft-ce là la recompēfe, que vous me donnez, pour vous auoir fi tendrement aymé ? Mais il n'importe, je fuis refoluë à vous adorer toute ma vie, & à ne voir jamais personne ; & je vous affeure que vous ferez bien auffi de n'aymer perfonne. Pourriez vous eftre content d'vne Paffion moins ardente que la miēne ? Vous trouuerez, peut-eftre, plus de beauté (vous m'auez pourtant dit autrefois, que j'eftois affez belle) mais vous ne trouuerez jamais tant d'amour, & tout le refte n'eft rien. Ne rempliffez plus vos lettres de chofes inutiles, & ne m'efcriuez plus de me fouuenir de vous ? Ie ne puis vous oublier, & je n'oublie pas auffi, que vous m'auez fait efperer, que vous viēdriez passer quelque temps auec moy. Helas! pourquoy n'y voulez vous pas paffer toute voftre vie ? S'il m'eftoit poffible de fortir de ce malheureux Cloiftre, je n'attendrois pas en Portugal l'effet de vos promeffes : j'irois, fans garder aucune mefure, vous chercher, vous fuiure, & vous aymer par tout le monde : je n'ofe me flater que cela puiffe eftre, je ne veux point nourrir vne efperance, qui me donneroit affeurément quelque plaifir, & je ne veux plus eftre fenfible qu'aux douleurs. I'auouë cependant que l'occafion, que mon frere m'a donnée de vous efcrire, a furpris en moy quelques mouuemens de joye, & qu'elle a fufpendu pour vn moment le defefpoir, où je fuis. Ie vous coniure de me dire, pourquoy vous vous eftes attaché à m'enchanter, comme vous auez fait, puifque vous fçauiez bien que vous deuiez m'abandonner ? Et pourquoy auez vous efté fi acharné à me rendre malheureufe ? que ne me laiffiez vous en repos dans mon Cloiftre ? vous auois-ie fait quelque iniure ? Mais ie vous demande pardon : ie ne vous im-

LETTRES TRADVITES

PREMIERE LETTRE pute rien : ie ne fuis pas en eftat de penfer à ma vengeance, & i'accufe feulement la rigueur de mon Deftin. Il me femble quen nous feparant, il nous a fait tout le mal, que nous pouuiōs craindre ; il ne fçauroit feparer nos cœurs ; l'amour qui eft plus puiffant que luy, les a vnis pour toute noftre vie. Si vous prenez quelque intereft à la mienne, efcriuez moy fouuent. Ie merite bien que vous preniez quelque foin de m'apprendre l'eftat de voftre cœur, & de voftre fortune, fur tout venez, me voir. Adieu, ie ne puis quitter ce papier, il tombera entre vos mains, ie voudrois bien auoir le mefme bon-heur : Helas ! infenfée que ie fuis, ie m'apperçois bien que cela n'eft pas poffible. Adieu, ie n'en puis plus. Adieu, aymez moy toûjours ; & faites moy fouffrir encore plus de maux.

SECONDE LETTRE

IL me ſemble que je fais le plus grād tort du monde aux ſentimēs de mon cœur, de taſcher de vous les faire connoiſtre en les écriuant: que je ferois heureuſe, ſi vous en pouuiez biē iuger par la violence des voſtres! mais ie ne dois pas m'en rapporter à vous, & ie ne puis m'empeſcher de vous dire, bien moins vivement, que je ne le ſens, que vous ne devriez pas me mal-traitter, comme vous faites, par vn oubly, qui me met au deſeſpoir, & qui eſt meſme honteux pour vous; il eſt bien iuste au moins, que vous ſouffriez que ie me plaigne des malheurs, que i'avois bien preveus, quand ie vous vis resolu de me quitter ie connois bien que ie me ſuis abuſeé lorſque i'ay penſé, que vous auriez

LETTRES TRADVITES

SECONDE LETTRE

vn procedé de meilleure foy, qu'on n'a accouſtumé d'auoir, parce que l'excez de mon amour me mettoit, ce ſemble, au deſſus de toutes ſortes de ſoupçons, & qu'il meritoit plus de fidelité, qu'on n'en trouue d'ordinaire : mais la diſpoſitiō, que vous auez à me trahir, l'emporte enfin ſur la juſtice, que vous deuez à tout ce que i'ay fait pour vous, ie ne laiſſerois pas d'eſtre bien malheureuſe, ſi vous ne m'aymiez, que parce que ie vous ayme, & ie voudrois tout deuoir à voſtre ſeule inclination mais ie ſuis ſi éloignée d'eſtre en cét eſtat, que ie n'ay pas receu vne ſeule lettre de vous depuis ſix mois : j'attribuë tout ce mal-heur à l'aueuglement, auec lequel ie me ſuis abandonnée à m'attacher à vous : ne deuois-je pas preuoir que mes plaiſirs finiroient plûtoſt que mon amour ? pouuois-ie eſperer, que vous demeureriez toute voſtre vie en Portugal, & que vous renonceriez à voſtre fortune & à voſtre Pays, pour ne penſer qu' à moy ? mes douleurs ne peuuent receuoir aucun ſoulagement, & le ſouuenir de mes plaiſirs me comble de deſeſpoir : Quoy ! tous mes deſirs ſeront donc inutiles, & ie ne vous verray iamais en ma chambre avec toute l'ardeur, & tout l'emportement, que vous me faifiez voir? mais helas! je m'abufe, & je ne connois que trop, que tous les mouuemens, qui occupoient ma tefte, & mon cœur, n'eftoient excitez en vous, que par quelques plaifirs, & qu'ils finiffoient auffitost qu'eux; il falloit que dans ces momens trop heureux j'appellaffe ma raifon à mon fecours pour moderer l'excez funefte de mes delices, & pour m'annoncer tout ce que ie fouffre prefentement: mais ie me donnois toute à vous, & ie n'eftois pas en eftat de penser à ce qui eût pû empoifonner ma ioye, & m'empefcher de ioüyr pleinement des témoignages ardens de voftre paffion; ie m'apperceuois trop agreablement que i'eftois auec vous pour penfer que vous feriez vn iour éloigné de moy: ie me fouuiens pourtant de vous auoir dit quelquefois que vous me rendriez malheureuse: mais ces frayeurs eftoient bien-toft diffipées, & ie prenois plaifir, à vous les facrifier, & à m'abandonner à l'enchantement, & à la mauuaise foy de vos protestations: ie voy bien le remede à tous mes maux, & i'en ferois bien-toft déliurée fi ie

SECONDE LETTRE ne vous aymois plus : mais, helas ! quel remède ; non i'ayme mieux fouffrir encore dauantage, que vous oublier. Helas ! cela dépend il de moy ? Ie ne puis me reprocher d'auoir fouhaité vn feul moment de ne vous plus aymer : vous eftes plus à plaindre ; que je ne fuis, & il vaut mieux fouffrir tout ce que je fouffre, que de ioüir des plaifirs languifans, que vous donnent vos Maitreffes de France : ie n'enuie point voftre indifference, & vous me faites pitié : Ie vous défie de m'oublier entierement : Ie me flatte de vous auoir mis en eftat de n'auoir fans moy, que des plaifirs imparfaits, & ie fuis plus heureufe que vous, puifque ie fuis plus occupée. L'on m'a fait depuis peu Portiere en ce Conuent : tous ceux qui me parlent, croyent que ie fois fole, ie ne fçay ce que ie leur répons : Et il faut que les Religieufes foyent auffi infenfées que moy, pour m'auoir crû capable de quelque foin. **Deux petits laquais Portugais.** Ah ! i'enuie le bon-heur d'Emanuel, & de Francifque ; pourquoy ne fuis-je pas inceffamment auec vous, comme eux ? ie vous aurois fuiuy, & ie vous aurois affeurément feruy de meilleur cœur, ie ne fouhaite rien en ce mōde, que vous voir ; au moins fouuenez vous de moy ? ie me contente de vostre fouuenir : mais ie n'ofe m'en affeurer ; ie ne bornois pas mes efperances à voftre fouuenir, quād ie vous voyois tous les iours : mais vous m'auez bien apris, qu'il faut que ie me foûmette à tout ce que vous voudrez : cependāt ie ne me repēs point de vous auoir adoré, ie fuis bien-aife, que vous m'ayez feduite : voftre abfence rigoureufe, & peut-eftre éternelle, ne diminuë en rien l'emportement de mon amour : ie veux que tout le mond le fçache, ie n'en fais point vn myftere, & ie fuis rauie d'auoir fait tout ce que i'ay fait pour vous contre toute forte de bien-feance : ie ne mets plus mon honneur, & ma religion qu'à vous aymer éperdüement toute ma vie, puifque i'ay commencé à vous aymer : ie ne vous dis point toutes ces chofes, pour vous obliger à m'efcrire. Ah ! ne vous contraignez point ; ie ne veux de vous, que ce qui viendra de voftre mouuement, & ie refufe tous les témoignages de voftre amour dont vous pourriez vous empefcher : j'auray du plaifir à vous excufer, parce

SECONDE LETTRE

LETTRES TRADVITES

SECONDE
LETTRE

que vous aurez, peut-eftre, du plaifir à ne pas prendre la peine de m'écrire : & ie fens vne profonde difpofition à vous pardonner toutes vos fautes. Vn Officier François a eu la charité de me parler ce matin plus de trois heures de vous, il m'a dit que la paix de France, eftoit faite : fi cela eft, ne pourriez vous pas me venir voir, & m'emmener en Frāce ? Mais ie ne le merite pas, faites tout ce qu'il vous plaira, mon amour ne depend plus de la maniere, dont vous me traiterez ; depuis que vous eftes party, je n'ay pas eu vn feul moment de fanté, & je n'ay aucun plaifir qu'en nomment voftre nō mille fois le iour ; quelques Religieufes, qui fçauent l'eftat deplorable, où vous m'auez plongée, me parlent de vous fort fouuent : je sors le moins qu'il m'eft poffible de ma chambre, où vous eftes venu tant de fois, & ie regarde fans ceffe vôtre portrait, qui m'eft mille fois plus cher que ma vie, il me donne quelque plaifir : mais il me donne auffi bien de la douleur, lors que ie penfe que ie ne vous reuerray, peut-eftre jamais ; pourquoy faut-il qu'il foit poffible que ie ne vous verray, peut-eftre,

EN FRANÇOIS

iamais? M'auez vous pour toûjours abandonnée? Ie ſuis au deſeſpoir, voſtre pauure Mariane n'en peut plus, elle s'éuanoüit en finiſſant cette Lettre. Adieu, adieu, ayez pitié de moy.

SECONDE LETTRE

TROISIESME LETTRE

Q V'eſt-ce que je deuiendray, & qu'eſt-ce que vous voulez que ie faſſe? Ie me trouue bien éloignée de tout ce que j'auois preueu : l'eſperois que vous m'écririez de tous les endroits, où vous paſſeriez, & que vos lettres feroient fort longues ; que vous fouſtiēdrez ma Paſſion par l'eſperance de vous reuoir, qu'vne entiere confiance en voſtre fidelité me donneroit quelque forte de repos, & que ie demeurerois cependant dans vn eſtat aſſez fupportable fans d'extrèmes douleurs : j'auois mefme penſê à quelques foibles projets de faire tous les efforts dont ie ferois capable, pour me guerir, fi ie pouuois connoiſtre bien certainement que vous m'euſſiez tout a fait oubliée ; voſtre éloignement, quelques mouuemens de deuotiō ; la crainte de ruiner entierement le reſte de ma ſanté par tant de veilles, & par tant d'inquietudes ; le peu d'apparence de voſtre retour : la froideur de voſtre Paſſion, & de vos derniers adieux ; voſtre depart, fondé ſur d'aſſez meſchās pretextes, & mille autres raiſons, qui ne ſont que trop bonnes, & que trop inutiles, ſembloient me promettre vn ſecours aſſez aſſeuré, s'il me deuenoit neceſſaire : n'ayant enfin à combatre que contre moy meſme, ie ne pouuois jamais me défier de toutes mes ſoibleſſes, ny apprehender tout ce que ie ſouffre aujourd'huy. Helas ! que ie ſuis à plaindre, de ne partager pas mes douleurs auec vous, & d'eſtre toute ſeule malheureuſe : cette penſée me tuë, & je meurs de frayeur, que vous n'ayez iamais eſté extrémement ſenſible à tous nos plaiſirs : Oüy, ie connois preſentement la mauuaiſe foy de tous vos mouuemens : vous m'auez trahie toutes les fois, que vous m'auez dit, que vous eſtiez rauy d'eſtre ſeul auec moy ; ie ne dois qu'a mes importunitez vos empreſſemens, & vos tranſports ; vous auiez fait de ſens froid vn deſſein de m'enflamer, vous n'auez regardé ma Paſſion que comme

TROISIESME LETTRE vne victoire, & voftre cœur n'en a jamais efté profondement touché, n'eftes vous pas bien malheureux, & n'auez vous pas bien peu de delicateffe, de n'auoir fçeu profiter qu'en cette maniere de mes emportemens? Et comment eft-il poffible qu'auec tant d'amour ie n'aye pû vous rendre tout a fait heureux? ie regrette pour l'amour de vous feulement les plaifirs infinis, que vous auez perdus: faut-il que vous n'ayez pas voulu en ioüir? Ah! fi vous les cōnoiffiez, vous trouueriez fans doute qu'ils font plus fenfibles, que celuy de m'auoir abufée, & vous auriez efprouué, qu'on eft beaucoup plus heureux, & qu'on fent quelque chofe de bien plus touchant, quand on ayme violamment, que lors'qu'on eft aymé. Ie ne fçay, ny ce que ie fuis, ny ce que ie fais, ny ce que ie defire : ie fuis defchirée par mille mouuemens contraires : Peut-on s'imaginer vn eftat fi deplorable? Ie vous ayme éperduëment, & ie vous mefnage affez pour n'ofer, peut-eftre, fouhaiter que vous foyez agité des mefmes tranfports : ie me tuërois, ou ie mourrois de douleur fans me tuër, fi j'eftois affeurée que vous

EN FRANÇOIS

n'auez jamais aucun repos, que voſtre vie n'eſt que trouble, & qu'agitation, que vous pleurez ſans ceſſe, & que tout vous eſt odieux ; je ne puis ſuffire à mes maux, comment pourrois-je ſupporter la douleur, que me donneroient les voſtres, qui me feroient mille fois plus ſenſibles ? Cependant ie ne puis auſſi me refoudre à defirer que vous ne penſiez point à moy ; & à vous parler ſincerement, ie fuis ialouſe auec fureur de tout ce qui vous donne de la joye, & qui touche voſtre cœur, & voſtre gouſt en France. Ie ne ſçay pourquoy ie vous écris, ie voy bien que vous aurez ſeulement pitié de moy, & ie ne veux point de voſtre pitié ; j'ay bien du depit côtre moy-meſme, quand ie fais reflexion ſur tout ce que ie vous ay ſacrifié : j'ay perdu ma reputation, je me ſuis expoſée à la fureur de mes parens, à la feverité des loix de ce Païs contre les Religieuſes, & à voſtre ingratitude, qui me paroiſt le plus grand de tous les malheurs : cependant je fens bien que mes remors ne font pas veritables, que ie voudrois du meilleur de mon cœur, auoir couru pour l'amour de vous de plus grans dangers,

TROISIESME
LETTRE

LETTRES TRADVITES

TROISIESME LETTRE & que i'ay vn plaiſir funeste d'auoir hazardé ma vie & mō honneur, tout ce que i'ay de plus precieux, ne devoit-il pas eſtre en voſtre diſpoſition ? Et ne dois-je pas eſtre bien aiſe de l'auoir employé, comme i'ay fait : il me ſemble meſme que ie ne ſuis gueres contente ny de mes douleurs, ny de l'excez de mon amour, quoi que ie ne puiſſe, helas ! me flater aſſez pour être contente de vous ; je vis, infidelle que ie suis, & ie fais autant de choſes pour conſerver ma vie, que pour la perdre, Ah ! j'en meurs de honte : mon deſeſpoir n'eſt donc que dans mes Lettres ? Si je vous aimois autant que ie vous l'ay dit mille fois, ne ferois-je pas morte, il y a long-temps ? Ie vous ay trompé, c'eſt à vous à vous plaindre de moy : Helas ! pourquoy ne vous en plaignez vous pas ? Ie vous ay veu partir, ie ne puis eſperer de vous voir iamais de retour, & ie reſpire cependant : ie vous ay trahy, ie vous en demande pardon : mais ne me l'accordez pas ? Traittez moy feueremēt ? Ne trouuez point que mes ſentimens ſoient aſſez violens ? Soyez plus difficile à contēter ? Mandez moy que vo' voulez

EN FRANÇOIS

que ie meure d'amour pour vous ? Et TROISIESME
ie vous conjure de me donner ce fecours, LETTRE
afin que ie furmonte la foibleffe de mon
fexe, & que ie finiffe toutes mes irrefolu-
tions par vn veritable defefpoir ; vne fin
tragique vo' obligeroit fans doute à
penfer fouuent à moy, ma memoire vous
feroit chere, & vous feriez, peut-eftre,
fenfiblement touché d'vne mort extraordinaire, ne vaut-elle pas mieux que
l'eftat, où vous m'auez reduite ? Adieu,
ie voudrois bien ne vous auoir iamais
veu. Ah ! ie fens viuement la .fauffeté
de ce fentiment, & ie connois dans le
moment que ie vous écris, que i'aime
bien mieux eftre malheureufe en vo'
aimant, que de ne vous auoir iamais
veu ; je confens donc fans murmure à
ma mauuaife deftinée, puifque vous
n'auez pas voulu la rendre meilleure.
Adieu, promettez moy de me regretter
tendrement, fi ie meurs de douleur, &
qu'au moins la violence de ma Paffion
vous donne du dégouft & de l'éloignement pour toutes chofes ; cette confola-
tion me fuffira, & s'il faut que ie vous
abandonne pour toûjours, ie voudrois
bien ne vous laiffer pas à vne autre.

LETTRES TRADVITES

TROISIESME LETTRE Ne feriez vous pas bien cruel de vous feruir de mon defefpoir, pour vous rendre plus aimable, & pour faire voir, que vous auez donné la plus grande Paffion du monde ? Adieu encore vne fois, ie vous écris des lettres trop longues, je n'ay pas affez d'égard pour vous, ie vous en demande pardon, & j'ofe efperer que vous aurez quelque indulgence pour vne pauure infenfée, qui ne l'eftoit pas, comme vous fçauez, auant qu'elle vous aimât. Adieu, il me femble que ie vous parle trop fouuent de l'eftat infuportable où ie fuis : cependant ie vous remercie dans le fonds de mon cœur du defefpoir, que vous me caufez, & ie detefte la tranquillité, où j'ay vefcu, auant que je vous connuffe. Adieu, ma Paffion augmente à chaque moment. Ah ! que j'ay de chofes à vous dire.

QVATRIESME LETTRE

Vostre Lieutenant vient de me dire, qu'vne tempeste vous a obligé de relafcher au Royaume d'Algarve : je crains que vous n'ayez beaucoup souffert sur la mer, & cette apprehension m'a tellement occupée ; que je n'ay plus pensé à tous mes maux, estes vous bien persuadé que vostre Lieutenant prenne plus de part que moy à tout ce qui vous arriue? Pourquoy en est-il mieux informé, & enfin pourquoi ne m'auez vous point écrit ? Ie suis bien malheureuse, si vous n'en aués trouué aucune occasion depuis vostre depart, & ie la suis bien dauantage, si vous en aués trouué sans m'écrire ; vostre injustice & vostre ingratitude sont extrémes : mais ie serois au desespoir, si elles vous attiroient quelque

QVATRIESME LETTRE malheur, & j'aime beaucoup mieux qu'elles demeurent fans punition, que fi j'en eftois vangeé : je refifte à toutes les apparences, qui me deuroient perfuader, que vous ne m'aimés gueres, & ie fens bien plus de difpofition à m'abandonner aueuglement à ma Paffion, qu'aux raifons, que vo' me donnez de me plaindre de voftre peu de foin : que vous m'auriés épargné d'inquietudes, fi voftre procedé euft efté auffi languiffant les premiers jours, que je vous vis, qu'il m'a parû depuis quelque temps ! mais qui n'auroit efté abufeé, comme moy, par tant d'empreffement, & à qui n'euffent-ils paru finceres ? Qu'on a de peine à fe refoudre à foupçonner longtemps la bonne foy de ceux qu'on aime ! ie voy bien que la moindre excufe vous fuffit, & fans que vous preniez le foin de m'en faire, l'amour que i'ay pour vous, vous fert fi fidelemēt, que ie ne puis confentir à vo' trouuer coupable, que pour joüir du fenfible plaifir de vous juftifier moy-même. Vous m'auez confommée par vos affiduitez, vous m'auez enflamée par vos tranfports, vo' m'auez charmée par vos complaifances, vous m'auez affeurée par vos

EN FRANÇOIS

QUATRIESME LETTRE

fermens, mon inclinatiō violente m'a feduite, & les fuites de ces commencemēs fi agreables, & fi heureux ne font que des larmes, que des foûpirs, & qu'vne mort funefte, fans que ie puiffe y porter aucun remede. Il eft vray que i'ay eu des plaifirs bien furprenans en vous aimant : mais ils me couftent d'eftranges douleurs, & tous les mouuemēs, que vous me caufez, font extrémes. Si i'auois refifté auec opiniâtreté à voftre amour, fi je vous auois donné quelque fujet de chagrin, & de jaloufie pour vous enflamer dauantage, fi vous auiez remarqué quelque mefnagement artificieux dans ma conduite, fi i'auois enfin voulu oppofer ma raifon à l'inclination naturelle que j'ay pour vous, dont vo' me fiftes bien-toft apperceuoir (quoy que mes efforts euffent efté fans doute inutiles) vous pourriez me punir feuerement, & vous feruir de voftre pouuoir : mais vous me paruftes aimable, auant que vous m'euffiez dit, que vous m'aimiez, vous me témoignaftes vne grande Paffion, j'en fûs rauie, & ie m'abandonnay à vous aimer éperduëment, vous n'eftiés point aueuglé, comme moy, pour-quoy aués

LETTRES TRADVITES

QVATRIESME LETTRE vo' donc fouffert que ie deuinffe en l'eftat où ie me trouue ? qu'eft-ce que vous vouliez faire de tous mes emportemens, qui ne pouuoient vous eftre que tres-importuns ? Vous fçauiez bien que vous ne feriez pas toûjours en Portugal, & pourquoy m'y aués vous voulu choifir pour me rendre fi malheureufe, vous euffiés trouué fans doute en ce Païs quelque femme qui euft efté plus belle, auec laquelle vous euffiés eu autant de plaifir, puifque vous n'en cherchiés que de groffiers, qui vo' eut fidelement aimé auffi long-temps qu'elle vous eut veu, que le temps euft pû confoler de voftre abfence, & que vous auriés pû quitter fans perfidie, & fans cruauté : ce procedé eft biē plus d'vn Tyran, attaché à perfe-cuter, que d'vn Amant, qui ne doit penfer qu'à plaire ; Helas ! Pourquoy exercés vous tant de rigueur fur vn cœur, qui eft à vous ? Ie voy bien que vous eftes auffi facile à vous laiffer perfuader contre moy, que ie l'ay efté à me laiffer per-suader en voftre faueur ; j'aurois refifté, fans auoir befoin de tout mon amour, & fans m'apperceuoir que j'euffe rien fait d'extraordinaire, à de plus grandes

EN FRANÇOIS

raiſons, que ne peuuēt eſtre celles, qui vo' ont obligé à me quitter : elles m'euſſent parû bien foibles, & il n'y en a point, qui euſſent jamais pû m'arracher d'aupres de vous : mais vous aués voulu profiter des pretextes, que vous aués trouués de retourner en Frāce ; vn vaiſſeau partoit, que ne le laiſſiés vous partir ? voſtre famille vous auoit eſcrit, ne ſçaués vous pas toutes les perſecutions, que j'ay ſouffertes de la mienne ? Voſtre hōneur vous engageoit à m'abandonner, ay-je pris quelque ſoin du mien ? Vous eſtiés obligé d'aller ſeruir voſtre Roy, ſi tout ce qu'on dit de luy, eſt vray, il n'a aucun beſoin de voſtre ſecours, & il vous auroit excuſé ; j'euſſe eſté trop heureuſe, ſi nous auions paſſé noſtre vie enſemble : mais puiſqu'il falloit qu'vne abſence cruelle nous ſeparât, il me ſemble que je dois eſtre bien aiſe de n'auoir pas eſté infidele, & ie ne voudrois pas pour toutes les choſes du mōde, auoir commis vne aĉtion ſi noire : Quoy ! vous auez connu le fonds de mon cœur, & de ma tendreſſe, & vous auez pû vous reſoudre à me laiſſer pour iamais, & à m'expoſer aux frayeurs, que ie dois auoir, que vous ne vous ſouue-

QVATRIESME LETTRE

LETTRES TRADVITES

QVATRIESME
LETTRE

nez plus de moy, que pour me facrifier à vne nouuelle Paffion ? Ie voy bien que ie vous aime, comme vne folle : cependant ie ne me plains point de toute la violence des mouuemens de mō cœur, ie m'accouftume à fes perfecutions, & ie ne pourrois viure fans vn plaifir, que ie defcouure, & dont ie joüis en vous aimāt au milieu de mille douleurs : mais ie fuis fans ceffe perfecutée auec un extréme defagréemēt par la haine, & par le dégouftt que j'ay pour toutes chofes ; ma famille, mes amis & ce Conuent me font infuportables ; tout ce que ie fuis obligeé de voir, et tout ce qu'il faut que ie faffe de toute neceffité, m'eft odieux : je fuis fi jaloufe de ma Paffion, qu'il me femble que toutes mes actions, & que tous mes deuoirs vous regardent : Oüy, ie fais quelque fcrupule, fi ie n'employe tous les momens de ma vie pour vous ; que ferois-je, helas ! fans tant de haine, & fans tant d'amour, qui rempliffent mon cœur ? Pourrois-je furviure à ce qui m'occupe inceffamment, pour mener vne vie tranquille & languiffante ? Ce vuide & cette infenfibilité ne peuuent me conuenir. Tout le monde s'est apperceu du changement entier de mon humeur, de mes manieres, & de ma persōne, ma Mere m'en a parlé auec aigreur, & enfuite auec quelque bonté, ie ne fçay ce que ie luy ay répondu, il me femble que ie luy ay tout auoüé. Les Religieufes les plus feueres ont pitié de l'eftat où je fuis, il leur donne mefme quelque confideration, & quelque menagemēt pour moy; tout le monde eft touché de mon amour. & vo' demeurez dans vne profonde indiference, fans m'efcrire, que des lettres froides; pleines de redites; la moitié du papier n'eft pas remply, & il paroift groffierement que vous mourez d'enuie de les auoir acheuées. Dona Brites me perfecuta ces jours paffez pour me faire fortir de ma chambre, & croyant me diuertir, elle me mena promener fur le Balcon, d'où l'on voit Mertola, je la fuiuis, & je fûs auffi-toft frapée d'vn fouuenir cruel, qui me fit pleurer tout le refte du jour : elle me ramena, & ie me jettay fur mon lict, où ie fis mille réflexions fur le peu d'apparence, que ie voy de guerir jamais : ce qu'on fait pour me foulager, aigrit ma douleur, & ie

LETTRES TRADVITES

QVATRIESME LETTRE trouue dans les remedes mefmes des raifons particulieres de m'afliger : je vous ay veu fouuent paffer en ce lieu auec vn air, qui me charmoit, & j'eſtois fur ce Balcon le jour fatal, que ie cōmençay à fentir les premiers effets de ma Paffion malheureufe : il me fembla que vous vouliez me plaire, quoy que vous ne me connuffiez pas : je me perfuaday que vous m'auiez remarquée entre toutes celles, qui eftoient auec moy, ie m'imaginay que lors que vous vous arreftiez, vous eftiez bien aife, que ie vous viffe mieux, & i'admiraffe voſtre adreffe, & voftre bonne grace, lors que vous pouffiez vôtre cheual, i'eſtois furprife de quelque frayeur, lors que vous le faifiez paffer dans vn endroit difficile : enfin je m'intereffois fecrettement à toutes vos actions, je fentois bien que vous ne m'eftiez point indifferent, & ie prenois pour moy tout ce que vous faifiez : vous ne connoiffez que trop les fuites de ces commencemens, & quoy que ie n'aye rien à mefnager, ie ne dois pas vous les efcrire, de crainte de vous rendre plus coupable, s'il eft poffible que vous ne l'eſtes, & d'auoir à me reprocher tant

EN FRANÇOIS

QVATRIESME LETTRE

d'efforts inutiles pour vous obliger à m'eſtre fidele, vous ne le ferez point : Puis-je eſperer de mes lettres & de mes reproches ce que mon amour & mon abandonnement n'ont pû ſur voſtre ingratitude ? Ie ſuis trop aſſeurée de mon malheur, voſtre procedé injuſte ne me laiſſe pas la moindre raiſon d'en douter, & ie dois tout apprehender, puiſque vous m'auez abandonée. N'aurez vous de charmes que pour moy, & ne paroiſtrez vous pas agreable à d'autres yeux ? Ie croy que ie ne ſeray pas fâchée que les ſentimens des autres iuſtifient les miens en quelque façon, & ie voudrois que toutes les femmes de France vous trouuaſſent aimable, qu'aucune ne vous aimât, & qu'aucune ne vous plût : ce projet eſt ridicule, & impoſſible : neantmoins j'ay aſſez éprouué que vous n'eſtes gueres capable d'vn grand enteſtement, & que vous pourrez bien m'oublier ſans aucun ſecours, & ſans y eſtre contraint par vne nouuelle Paſſion : peut-eſtre, voudrois-je que vous euſſiez quelque pretexte raiſonnable ? Il eſt vray, que ie ſerois plus malheureuſe, mais vous ne ſeriez pas ſi coupable : je voy bien que vovs

LETTRES TRADVITES

QVATRIESME LETTRE demeurerez en Frāce fans de grands plaifirs, auec vne entiere liberté ; la fatigue d'vn long voyage, quelque petite bien-feance, & la crainte de ne répondre pas à mes tranfports, vous retiennent : Ah ! ne m'apprehendez point ? Ie me contenteray de vous voir de temps en temps, & de fçauoir feulement que no' fommes en mefme lieu : mais ie me flatte, peut-eftre, & vous ferez plus touché de la rigueur & de la feuerité d'vne autre, que vous ne l'auez efté de mes faueurs ; eft-il poffible que vous ferez enflammé par de mauuais traittemens ? Mais auant que de vous engager dans vne grande Paffion, penfez bien à l'excez de mes douleurs, à l'incertitude de mes projets, à la diuerıité de mes mouuemens, à l'extrauagance de mes Lettres, à mes confiances, à mes defefpoirs, à mes fouhaits, à ma jaloufie ? Ah ! vous allez vous rendre malheureux ; je vous conjure de profiter de l'eftat où ie fuis, & qu'au moins ce que ie fouffre pour vous, ne vous foit pas inutile ? Vous me fites, il y a cinq ou fix mois vne fafcheufe confidēce, & vo' m'auoüâtes de trop bonne foy, que vous auiez aimé vne

EN FRANÇOIS

Dame en voſtre Païs : ſi elle vous em-pefche de reuenir, mādez-le moy ſans ménagement ? afin que ie ne languiſſe plus ? quelque reſte d'eſperance me ſouſtiēt encore, & ie ſeray bien aiſe (ſi elle ne doit auoir aucune ſuite) de la perdre tout à fait, & de me perdre moy-meſme ; enuoyez moy ſon portrait auec quelqu'vne de ſes Lettres ? Et eſcriuez moy tout ce qu'elle vous dit ? I'y trou-uerois, peut-eſtre, des raiſons de me conſoler, ou de m'affliger dauantage, ie ne puis demeurer plus long-temps dās l'eſtat où ie ſuis, & il n'y a point de chāgement, qui ne me ſoit fauorable : Ie voudrois auſſi auoir le portrait de voſtre frere & de voſtre Belle-ſœur : tout ce qui vous eſt quelque choſe, m'eſt fort cher, & ie ſuis entierement deuoüée à ce qui vous touche : je ne me ſuis laiſſé aucune diſpoſition de moy-meſme ; Il y a des momens, où il me ſemble que j'aurois aſſez de soûmiſſion pour ſeruir celle, que vous aimez ; vos mauuais traittemēs, & vos mépris m'ont tellement abatuë, que ie n'oſe quelque fois penſer ſeulement, qu'il me ſemble que ie pourrois eſtre jalouſe ſans vous déplaire, & que

QVATRIESME LETTRE

LETTRES TRADVITES

QVATRIESME LETTRE ie croy auoir le plus grand tort du monde de vous faire des reproches : je fuis fouuent conuaincuë, que ie ne dois point vous faire voir auec fureur, comme ie fais, des fentimens, que vo' defauoüez. Il y a long-temps qu'vn Officier attend voftre Lettre, i'auois refolu de l'efcrire d'vne maniere à vo' la faire receuoir fans dégouft : mais elle eft trop extrauagante, il faut la finir : Helas ! il n'eft pas en mon pouuoir de m'y refoudre, il me femble que je vous parle, quand ie vous efcris, & que vous m'eftes vn peu plus prefent ; La premiere ne fera pas fi longue, ny fi importune, vous pourrez l'ouurir & la lire fur l'affeurance, que ie vous donne, il eft vray que ie ne dois point vous parler d'vne paffion, qui vous déplaift, & ie ne vous en parleray plus. Il y aura vn an dans peu de jours que ie m'abandonnay toute à vous fans ménagement : voftre Paffion me paroiffoit fort ardente, & fort fincere, & ie n'euffe jamais penfé que mes faueurs vo' euffent affez rebuté, pour vous obliger à faire cinq cens lieuës, & à vous expofer à des naufrages, pour vo' en éloigner ; perfonne ne m'eftoit redeuable d'vn pareil

traittement : vous pouuez vous fouuenir QVATRIESME
de ma pudeur, de ma confufion & de LETTRE
mon defordre, mais vous ne vous fouuenez pas de ce qui vous engageroit à
m'aimer malgré vous. L'Officier, qui
doit vous porter cette Lettre, me mande
pour la quatrième fois, qu'il veut partir,
qu'il eft preffant, il abandonne fans doute
quelque malheureufe en ce Païs. Adieu,
j'ay plus de peine à finir ma Lettre, que
vo' n'en auez eu à me quitter, peut-eftre,
pour toûjours. Adieu, ie n'ofe vous
donner mille noms de tendreffe, ny
m'abandonner fans cōtrainte à tous mes
mouuemens : ie vo' aime mille fois plus
que ma vie, & mille fois plus que ie ne
penfe ; que vous m'eftes cher ! & que
vous m'eftes cruel ! vous ne m'efcriuez
point, ie n'ay pû m'empefcher de vo' dire
encore cela ; je vay recommencer, &
l'Officier partira ; qu'importe, qu'il parte,
j'écris plus pour moy, que pour vous, ie
ne cherche qu'à me foulager, auffi bien
la longueur de ma lettre vous fera peur,
vous ne la lirez point qu'eft-ce que
j'ay fait pour eftre fi malheureufe ?
Et pourquoy auez vous empoifonné
ma vie ? Que ne fuis-je née en vn

QVATRIESME LETTRE autre Païs. Adieu, pardonnez moy ? Ie n'ofe plus vous prier de m'aimer ; voyez où mon deftin m'a reduite ? Adieu.

CINQVIESME LETTRE

JE vous écris pour la derniere fois, & j'eſpere vous faire connoître par la differance des termes, & de la maniere de cette Lettre, que vous m'auez enfin perſuadée que vous ne m'aymiez plus, & qu'ainſi je ne dois plus vous aymer : Ie vous r'enuoyeray donc par la premiere voye tout ce qui me reſte encore de vous : Ne craignez pas que je vous écriue ; je ne mettray pas meſme voſtre nom audeſſus du pacquet ; j'ay chargé de tout ce détail Dona Brites, que j'auois accouſtumée à des confidences bien éloignées de celle-cy ; ſes ſoins me ſeront moins ſuſpects que les miens, elle prendra toutes les precautions neceſſaires, afin de pouuoir m'aſſeurer que vous auez receu le portrait & les bracelets que vous

CINQVIESME LETTRE m'auez donnés : Ie veux cependant que vous fçachiez que je me fens, depuis quelques jours, en eftat de brûler, & de déchirer ces gages de voftre Amour, qui m'eftoient fi chers, mais ie vous ay fait voir tant de foibleffe, que vous n'auriés jamais crû que j'euffe peu deuenir capable d'vne telle extremité, je veux donc joüir de toute la peine que j'ay euë à m'en feparer, & vous donner au moins quelque dépit : Ie vous aduoüe à ma honte & à la voftre, que ie me fuis trouuée plus attachée que ie ne veux vous le dire, à ces bagatelles, & que i'ay fenty que j'auois vn nouueau befoin de toutes mes reflexions, pour me défaire de chacune en particulier, lors mefme que ie me flattois de n'eftre plus attachée à vous : Mais on vient about de tout ce qu'on veut, auec tant de raifons : Ie les ay mifes entre les mains de Dona Brites ; que cette refolution ma coufté de larmes ! Apres mille mouuements & milles incertitudes que vous ne connoiffez pas, & dont ie ne vous rendray pas compte affurement. Ie l'ay coniurée de ne m'en parler iamais, de ne me les rēdre iamais, quand mefme ie les demanderois pour

EN FRANÇOIS

les reuoir encore vne fois, & de vous les renuoyer, enfin, fans m'en aduertir.

CINQVIESME LETTRE

Ie n'ay bien connû l'excés de mon Amour que depuis que i'ay voulu faire to' mes efforts pour m'en guerir, & ie crains que ie n'euffe ofé l'entreprendre, fi i'euffe pû préuoir tant de difficultées & tant de violences. Ie fuis perfuadée que j'euffe fenti des mouuemens moins defagreables en vo' aymant tout ingrat qve vous eftes, qu'en vous quittant pour toufiours. I'ay éprouué que vous m'eftiez moins cher que ma paffion, & j'ay eu d'eftranges peines à la combattre, apres que vos procedés iniurieux m'ont rendu voftre perfonne odieufe.

L'orgueil ordinaire de mon fexe ne m'a point aydé à prendre des refolutions contre vous; Helas! j'ay fouffert vos mepris, j'euffe fupporté vôtre haifne & toute la jaloufie que m'euft dōné l'attachement que vous euffiez peu auoir pour vn autre, j'aurois eu, au moins quelque paffion à combattre, mais voftre indifference m'eft infupportable; vos impertinantes proteftations d'amitié, & les ciuilités ridicules de voftre derniere lettre, m'ōt fait voir que vous auiez receu

# LETTRES TRADVITES

CINQVIESME LETTRE toutes celles que je vous ay écrites, qu'elles n'ont caufé dans voflre cœur aucun mouuement, & que cependant vous les auez luës : Ingrat, je fuis encore affez folle pour eftre au defefpoir de ne pouuoir me flatter quelles ne foient pas venuës jufques à vous, & qu'on ne vous les aye pas renduës ; Ie detefte voftre bonne foy, vous auois-je prié de me māder finceremēt la verité, que ne me laiffiez vous ma paffion ; vous n'auiez qu'à ne me point écrire ; ie ne cherchois pas à eftre éclaircie ; ne fuis-je pas bien malheureufe de n'auoir pû vous obliger à prēdre quelque foin de me tromper? & de n'eftre plus en eftat de vous excufer. Sçachez que je m'aperçois que vous eftes indigne de tous mes fentimens, & que je connois toutes vous méchantes qualitez : Cependāt (fi tout ce que j'ay fait pour vous peut meriter que vous ayez quelque petits égards pour les graces que ie vous demande) je vous coniure de ne m'écrire plus, & de m'ayder à vous oublier entierement, fi vous me témoigniez foiblement, mefme, que vous auez eu quelque peine en lisāt cette lettre, je

EN FRANÇOIS

vo' croirois peut-eſtre ; & peut-eſtre auſſi voſtre adueu & vôtre conſentement me donneroient du dépit & de la colere, & tout cela pourroit m'enflamer : Ne vous meſlez donc point de ma conduite, vous renuerſeriez, ſans doute, tous mes proiets, de quelque maniere que vous vouluſſiez y entrer ; je ne veux point ſçauoir le ſuccés de cette lettre ; ne troublés pas l'eſtat que ie me prepare, il me ſemble que vous pouuez eſtre content des maux que vous me cauſés (quelque deſſein que vous euſſiez fait de me rendre mal'heureuſe : Ne m'oſtez point de mon incertitude ; i'eſpere que j'en feray, auec le temps, quelque choſe de tranquille : Ie vous promets de ne vous point hayr, ie me défie trop des ſentimens violents, pour oſer l'entreprendre. Ie ſuis perſuadeé que ie trouuerois peut-eſtre, en ce pays vn Amant plus fidele & mieux fait ; mais helas ! qui pourra me donner de l'amour ? la paſſion d'vn autre m'occupera-t'elle ? La mienne a t'elle pû quelque choſe ſur vous ? N'éprouue-je pas qu'vn cœur attendry n'oublie jamais ce qui l'a fait apperceuoir des trāſports qu'il ne con-

CINQVIESME LETTRE

LETTRES TRADVITES

CINQVIESME LETTRE noiſſoit pas, & dont il eſtoit capable ; que tous ſes mouuemens ſont attachés à l'Idole qu'il s'eſt faite ; que ſes premieres idées & que ſes premieres bleſſures ne peuuent eſtre ny gueries ny effacées ; que toutes les paſſions qui s'offrent à ſon ſecours & qui font des efforts pour le remplir & pour le contenter, luy promettent vainement vne ſenſibilité qu'il ne retrouue plus, que tous les plaiſirs qu'il cherche ſans aucune enuie de les rencontrer, ne ſeruent qu'à luy faire bien connoître que rien ne luy eſt ſi cher, que le ſouuenir de ſes douleurs. Pourquoy m'auez vo' fait connoître l'imperfectiō & le deſagréement d'vn attachement qui ne doit pas durer eternellement, & les mal-heurs qui ſuiuent vn amour violent, lors qu'il n'eſt pas reciproque, & pourquoy vne inclinatiō aueugle & vne cruelle deſtineé s'attachent-elles, d'ordinaire, à nous déterminer pour ceux qui ſeroient ſenſibles pour quelque autre.

Quand meſme je pourrois eſperer quelque amuſemēt dans vn nouuel engagement, & que je trouuerois quelqu'vn de bonne foy, j'ay tant de pitié de moymeſme, que je ferois beaucoup de

EN FRANÇOIS

scrupule de mettre le dernier homme du monde en l'eſtat où vous m'auez reduite, & quoy que je ne ſois pas obligée à vous ménager ; je ne pourrois me reſoudre à exercer ſur vous, vne vengeance ſi cruelle, quand meſme elle dependeroit de moy, par vn changement que je ne preuois pas.

CINQVIESME LETTRE

Ie cherche dans ce moment à vous excuſer, & je cōprend bien qu'vne Religieuſe n'eſt guere aymable d'ordinaire : Cependant il ſemble que ſi on eſtoit capable de raiſons, dans les choix qu'on fait, on deueroit pluſtoſt s'attacher à elles qu'aux autres femmes, rien ne les empeſche de penſer inceſſāment à leur paſſion, elles ne ſont point détourneés par mille choſes qui diſſipent & qui occupent dans le monde, il me ſemble qu'il n'eſt pas fort agreable de voir celles qu'on ayme, touſiours diſtraites par mille bagatelles, & il faut auoir bien peu de delicateſſe, pour ſouffrir (ſans en eſtre au deſeſpoir) qu'elles ne parlent que d'aſſembleés, d'aiuſtements, & de promenades ; on eſt ſans ceſſe expoſé à de nouuelles jalouſies ; elles ſont obligeés à des égards, à des complaiſances, à des conuerſations : qui peut ſ'aſſeurer qu'elles

LETTRES TRADVITES

CINQVIESME LETTRE n'ont aucun plaifir dans toutes ces occafions, & qu'elles fouffrent toufiours leurs marys auec vn extrême dégouft, & fans aucun consentement; Ah qu'elles doiuent fe défier d'vn Amant qui ne leur fait pas rendre vn compte bien exaɛt là deffus, qui croit aisément & fans inquietude ce qu'elles luy difent, & qui les voit auec beaucoup de confiance & de tranquilité fuietes à tous ces deuoirs : Mais je ne pretens pas vous prouuer par de bonnes raifons, que vous deuiez m'aymer ; ce font de tres-méchans moyens, & j'en ay employé de beaucoup meilleurs qui ne m'ont pas reüffi ; je connois trop bien mon deftin pour tâcher à le furmonter ; je feray mal-heureufe toute ma vie ; ne l'éftois-je pas en vous voyāt tous les iours, je mourois de frayeur que vous ne me fuffiez pas fidel, je voulois vous voir à tous moments, & cela n'eftoit pas poffible, j'eftois troubleé par le peril que vous couriez en entrant dans ce Conuent; ie ne viuois pas lors que vous eftiez à l'armée, i'eftois au defefpoir de n'eftre pas plus belle & plus digne de vous, ie murmurois contre la mediocrité de ma condition, ie croyois fouuēt que l'attachement

EN FRANÇOIS

que vous paroiſſiez auoir pour moy, vous pourroit faire quelque tort, il me ſembloit que je ne vous aymois pas aſſez, j'apprehendois pour vous la colere de mes parents, & j'eſtois enfin dans vn eſtat auſſi pitoyable qu'eſt celuy où je ſuis preſentement ; ſi vous m'euſſiez donné quelques témoignages de voſtre paſſion depuis que vo' n'eſtes plus en Portugal ; j'aurois fait tous mes efforts pour en ſortir, je me fuſſe déguiſée pour vo' aller trouuer ; helas ! qu'eſt-ce que je fuſſe deuenuë, ſi vous ne vous fuſſiez plus ſouciée de moy, apres que j'euſſe eſté en France ; quel deſordre ? quel égarement ? quel cōble de honte pour ma famille, qui m'eſt fort chere depuis que je ne vous ayme plus. Vous voyez bien que je cōnnois de ſens froid qu'il eſtoit poſſible que je fuſſe encore plus à plaindre que ie ne ſuis ; & ie vous parle, au moins, raiſonnablement vne fois en ma vie ; que ma moderatiō vous plaira, & que vous ferez content de moy ; je ne veux point le fçauoir, je vous ay defia prié de ne m'écrire plus, & je vous en coniure encore.

N'auez vous jamais fait quelque re-

CINQVIESME LETTRE

CINQVIESME LETTRE flexion fur la maniere dont vous m'auez traitée, ne penfez vous iamais que vous m'auez plus d'obligation qu'à perfonne du monde ; je vous ay aymé comme vne incenfée ; que de mépris j'ay eu pour toutes chofes ! voftre procedé n'eft point d'vn honnefte homme, il faut que vous ayez eu pour moy de l'auerfion naturelle, puis que vous ne m'auez pas aymée éperduëment ; je me fuis laiffée enchanter par des qualitez tres-mediocres, qu'auez vous fait qui deuft me plaire ? quel facrifice m'auez vous fait ? n'auez vous pas cherché mille autres plaifirs ? auez vous renoncé au jeu, & à la chaffe ? n'eftes vous pas parti le premier pour aller à l'Armée ? n'en eftes-vous pas reuenu apres tous les autres, vous vous y eftes expofé folement, quoy que je vous euffe prié de vous ménager pour l'amour de moy, vous n'auez point cherché les moyens de vous eftablir en Portugal ? où vous eftiez eftimé ; vne lettre de voftre frere vous en a fait partir, fans hefiter vn moment, & n'ay-je pas fçeu que durant le voyage vous auez efté de la plus belle humeur du monde. Il faut aduoüer que ie fuis obligée à

EN FRANÇOIS

vous haïr mortellement ; ah ! ie me fuis attirée tous mes mal-heurs : je vous ay d'abord accouftumé à vne grande paffion, auec trop de bonne foy, & il faut de l'artifice pour fe faire aymer, il faut chercher auec quelque adreffe les moyens d'enflâmer, & l'amour tout feul ne donne point de l'amour, vous vouliez que ie vous aymaffe, & comme vous auiez formé ce deffein, il n'y a rien que vous n'euffiez fait pour y paruenir, vous vous fuffiez mefme refolu à m'aymer, s'il eut efté neceffaire ; mais vous auez connu que vous pouuiez reuffir dans voftre entreprife fans paffion, & que vous n'en auiez aucun befoin, quelle perfidie ? croyés vous auoir pû impunement me tromper, fi quelque hazard vous r'amenoit en ce pays, ie vous declare que ie vous liureray à la vengeance de mes parents. J'ay vécu long-temps dans vn abandonnement & dans vne idolatrie qui me donne de l'horreur, & mon remords me perfecute auec vne rigueur infupportable, ie fens viuement la honte des crimes que vo' m'auez fait com-mettre, & ie n'ay plus, helas ! la paffion qui m'empefchoit d'en connoiftre l'énor-

CINQVIESME LETTRE

CINQVIESME **LETTRE** mité ; quand eſt-ce que mon cœur ne fera plus dechiré ? quand eſt-ce que ie feray deliurée de cét embarras, cruel ! cependant je croy que ie ne vous fouhaitte point de mal, & que je me refouderois à confentir que vous fuſſiez heureux ; mais cōmēt pourrés vous l'eſtre ſi vous aués le cœur biē fait ; je veux vous écrire vne autre Lettre, pour vous faire voir que ie feray peut-eſtre plus tranquille dans quelque tēps ; que j'auray de plaiſir de pouuoir vous reprocher vos procedés iniuſtes aprés que ie n'en feray plus ſi viuement touchée, & lors que ie vous feray connoiſtre que ie vous mépriſe, que ie parle auec beaucoup d'indifference de voſtre trahiſon ; que j'ay oublié tous mes plaiſirs, & toutes mes douleurs, & que ie ne me fouuiens de vous que lors que ie veux m'en fouuenir. Ie demeure d'accord que vous auez de grands aduantages fur moy, & que vous m'auez donné vne paſſion qui ma fait perdre la raiſon, mais vous deuez en tirer peu de vanité ; j'eſtois jeune, j'eſtois credule, on m'auoit enfermée dans ce convēt depuis mon enfance, ie n'auois veu que des gens defagreables,

EN FRANÇOIS

CINQVIESME LETTRE

je n'auois jamais entendu les loüanges que vous me donniez inceffamment, il me fembloit que je vous deuois les charmes, & la beauté que vo' me trouuiez, & dont vous me faifiez apperceuoir, j'entendois dire du bien de vous, tout le monde me parloit en voftre faueur, vous faifiez tout ce qu'il falloit pour me donner de l'amour ; mais ie fuis, enfin, reuenuë de cét enchantement, vous m'auez dōné de grands fecours, & j'aduoüe que j'en auois vn extrême befoin : En vous renuoyant vos lettres, je garderay foigneufement les deux dernieres que vous m'auez écrites, & ie les reliray encore plus fouuent que ie n'ay leu les premieres, afin de ne retomber plus dans mes foibleffes, Ah! quelles me coûtēt cher, & que i'aurois efté heureufe, fi vous euffiez voulu fouffrir que ie vous euffe toûjours aimé. Ie connois bien que ie fuis encore vn peu trop occupée de mes reproches & de voftre infidelité ; mais fouuenez-vous que ie me fuis promife vn eftat plus paifible, & que j'y paruiendray, ou que ie prēdray contre moy quelque refolution extrême, que vous apprendrez fans beaucoup de

LETTRES TRADVITES

CINQVIESME LETTRE déplaifir ; mais ie ne veux plus rien de vous, ie fuis vne folle de redire les mefmes chofes fi fouuent, il faut vous quitter & ne penfer plus à vous, ie croy mefme que je ne vous écriray plus, fuis-je obligée de vous rendre vn compte exact de to' mes diuers mouuements.

FIN.

EXTRAIT DV
Priuilege du Roy

PAR Grace & Priuilege du Roy, donné à Paris le 28. jour d'Octobre 1668. Signé par le Roy en son Conseïl, MARGERET. Il est permis à CLAVDE BARBIN, Marchand Libraire, de faire imprimer vn Liure intitulé, *Lettres Portugaises*, pendant le temps & espace de *cinq anneés*; Et deffenses sont faites à tous autres de l'Imprimer, sur peine de quinze cent liures d'amande, de tous dépens, dommages & interests, comme il est plus amplement porté par lesdites Lettres de Priuilege.

Acheué d'imprimer pour la premiere fois le 4. Ianuier, 1669.

Les Exemplaires ont esté fournis.

Registré sur le Liure de la Communauté des Marchands Libraires & Imprimeurs de cette Ville, suiuant & conformement à l'Arrest de la Cour de Parlement du 8. Avril, 1653, aux charges & conditions portées par le present Priuilege. Fait à Paris le 17 Nouembre 1668. SOVBRON, Syndic.

BIBLIOGRAPHY

BIBLIOGRAPHY

THE following forms the English Bibliography of the Letters :—

'Five | love-letters | from a | Nun | to a | Cavalier | .' Done out of French into English. (By) Ro L'Estrange. London 1678. pp. III-117, 12mo.

Here is the Preface :—

To the Reader. | You are to take this Translation very kind- | ly, for the Authour | of it has ventur'd his | Reputation to oblige | you : Ventur'd it | (I say) even in the very Attempt of Co | pying so Nice an | Original. It is, in French, one of the | most Artificial Pieces | perhaps of the Kind, | that is anywhere Ex- | tant : Beside the Pe- | culiar Graces, and | Felicities of that Lan- | guage ; in the matter | of an Amour, which | cannot be adopted | into any other | Tongue without Ex- | tream Force, and Affectation. There was | (it seems) an Intrigue | of Love carry'd on | betwixt a French offi- | cer, and a Nun in | Portugal. The Cava- | lier forsakes his Mis- | tress, and Returns | for France. The La- | dy expostulates the | Business in five Let- | ters of complaint, | which she sends af- | ter him ; and those | five Letters are here | at your Service. You |

BIBLIO-
GRAPHY

will find in them the | Lively Image of an | Extravagant, and an | Unfortunate Passion ; | and that a woman may | be Flesh and Bloud, in a | Cloyster, as well as in a | Palace.

'Five love-letters from a Nun to a Cavalier,' etc., etc., 1693. 16mo. (2nd edition.)

'Five love-letters from a Nun to a Cavalier,' etc. etc., 1701. 16mo. (3rd edition.)

* 'New Miscellaneous | Poems | with five | Love-Letters | from | a Nun to a Cavalier | . Done into Verse [.' The Second Edition. London 1713. With frontispiece. 16mo. The Letters occupy pp. 3-43 ; the date of the 1st edition is unknown.

'Letters | from a | Portuguese Nun | to | an Officer | in the | French Army.' | Translated by | W. R. Bowles, Esqre. London, 1808. 12mo., with frontispiece. pp. xvi-125. This includes the so-called Second Part of the Letters.

'Letters from a Portuguese Nun,' etc., etc., 1817. (2nd edition.)

'Letters from a Portuguese Nun,' etc., etc., 1828. (3rd edition.)

'The Love Letters of a | Portuguese Nun | being the letters written by Marianna | Alcaforado to Noël Bouton de Cha-milly, Count of St. Leger (later | Marquis of Chamilly) in | the year 1668.' | Translated by | R. H. | New York 1890. 12mo. 148 p.

PORTUGUESE NUN

'Five love-letters written by a Cavalier (the Chevalier Del) in answer to the five love-letters written to him by a Nun.' London 1694. 12mo.

BIBLIOGRAPHY

---

* 'Seven | Portuguese Letters; | being a | second part | to the | Five Love-Letters | from a | Nun | to a | Cavalier | .' London 1681. pp. iii-78. 8vo.

* 'Seven | Love-Letters | from a | Nun | to a | Cavalier,' | etc.. etc., 1693. Small 4to. (2nd edition.)

N.B.—The translations marked with an asterisk are not mentioned by Senhor Cordeiro in his Bibliography.

APPENDIX

APPENDIX

URING the passage of the present work through the press, Mr. York Powell was fortunate enough to acquire by purchase in Oxford a book not mentioned in any bibliographical dictionary, nor possessed by any of the chief English libraries, containing a translation into verse of the five Letters of the Portuguese Nun. On account of the rarity of the book, of which this is probably a unique copy, as well as of the curious rendering of the famous Letters, it seemed advisable to transcribe here all that concerned the love-lorn Marianna, which has therefore been done. It should perhaps be mentioned that every inquiry as to the author of this translation and the date of its first edition has proved fruitless.

The following is a description of the book in question—

New Miscellaneous
POEMS
With Five
Love-Letters
FROM
A 𝕹un to a 𝕮avalier.

Done into Verse.

Nil dulcius est istoc amare aut amari,
præter hoc ipsum amare & amari.

𝕿he 𝕾econd 𝕰dition.

London, Printed for W. MEARS, at the *Lamb* without *Temple-bar*. 1713.

LETTERS OF A NUN

One vol. in 16mo.

First comes the Preface, then a Table of Contents, and the title-page to the Letters, which runs,

Five | Love-Letters | From a | Nun | to | A Cavalier | Done into Verse | London | Printed in the Year 1713. |

The Letters take up pp. 3-43, after which is another title-page to the Miscellaneous Poems, then the Poems themselves follow, occupying pp. 47-129.

The frontispiece to the volume shows the Nun seated at a table in the act of writing; upon the table is a lighted candle, rosary and ink-pot, while the portrait of her lover hangs over some book-shelves. The engraving is unsigned, and seems to be different from any of those hitherto recorded.

LOVE-LETTERS

FROM

A NUN TO A CAVALIER

LETTER I

AH! the unhappy Joys which Love
    contains,
How short the Pleasures, and how
    long the Pains!
Curs'd be the treach'rous Hopes
    that drew me on,
And made me fondly to my Ruin run.
What I the Blessing of my Life design'd
Is now become the Torment of my Mind:
A Torment! which is equally as great
As is his Absence that doth it create.
Heav'ns! must this Absence then for ever last,
This Absence! which does all my comfort blast?
Must I no more enjoy the pleasing Light
That charm'd my Heart with Rapture and Delight?
Must I no more those lovely Eyes behold

LETTERS OF A NUN

Which have so oft their Master's Passion told? APPENDIX
Nor was I wanting in the same intent; Letter I
A thousand times my Eyes in Flashes sent
The Dictates of my Heart, and shew'd you what
  they meant.
But now they must be other ways employ'd :
When I reflect on what I have enjoy'd
Tears of their own accord in Streams will flow,
To think I'm scorned, and left by faithless you.

And yet my Passion does so far exceed
A vulgar Flame, that I with Pleasure bleed,
And doat upon the Torments which from you pro-
  ceed.
From the first moment I beheld your Face,
To you I dedicated all my Days :
Your Eyes at first an easie Conquest gain'd,
Which since they have but too too well maintain'd.
Your Name each Hour I constantly repeat;
But what's (alas !) the Comfort which I meet?
Nought but my wretched Fate's too true Advice,
Which whispers to me in such Words as these :
Ah ! Mariane, why do'st hope in vain
To see thy lovely Fugitive again?
The dear, false, cruel Man's for ever gone,
And thou, unhappy thou ! art left alone :
Gone is the Tyrant, slighting all thy Charms,
And longs to languish in another's Arms.
In vain you weep, in vain you sigh and mourn,
For he will never, never more return.
To fly from thee, he left his Downy Ease,
And scorn'd the Dangers of the raging Seas.

THE LETTERS OF A

APPENDIX
Letter I

In France, dissolv'd in Pleasures, now he lies,
And for new Beauties every moment dies;
The Joys which once he with such Ardour sought
Are now (alas!) all vanish'd and forgot;
Nor art Thou ever present in his Thought.——

But hold! my Passion hurries me too far,
And makes me think you falser than you are.
You've, sure, more Honour than to use me so
For what I have endur'd and done for you,
Forget me! 'tis impossible you shou'd;
Nay, I believe yot cannot if you wou'd.
My Case is bad enough without that Curse,
I need not find fresh Plagues to make it worse.
And when I think with how much care you strove
To let me see at first, your dawning Love;
When I reflect upon the Bliss it brought,
The Pleasure is too great to be forgot;
And I shou'd think I were ungrateful grown,
Should I not love you, tho' by you undone.——

Yet oh! the Mem'ry of my former Joys,
So hard's my Fate, my present Ease destroys.
'Tis strange that what gave such delight before,
Shou'd serve to make me now lament the more.——

A Thousand Passions, not to be exprest,
Your Letter rais'd in my distracted Breast;
My vanquish'd Senses from their Office fled,
A long time stupid on the ground I laid,
And since I've often wish'd I had been dead.
But I unhappily reviv'd again
To suffer greater Torment, greater Pain;

180

PORTUGUESE NUN

APPENDIX
Letter I

A Thousand Evils I each Day endure,
Which nothing but the Sight of you can cure;
Yet I submit, without repining too,
Because the ills I bear proceed from you.——

And 'tis because you know the Pow'r you have,
You use me thus, and make me such a Slave.
Oh! give me leave to speak———
Is this the Recompense you think is due,
To those that sacrifice their Lives for you?
Yet use me as you will, to my last Breath,
Tho' loath'd by you, I'll keep my plighted Faith.——

And did you understand what Pleasure lies
In being constant, you wou'd Change despise.
You'll never meet with one will prove so kind,
Tho' in another you more Beauty find.
Yet I can tell the time, tho' now 'tis gone,
(Poor as it is) when mine has pleas'd alone.——

You need not bid me keep you in my Mind,
I'm too much of myself to that inclin'd.
I can't forget you, nor those Hopes you give
Of your return, in Portugal to live.
Cou'd I from this unhappy Cloister break,
You thro' the Perils of the World I'd seek.
I'd follow where you went, without Regret,
And constantly upon your Fortune wait,
Think not I keep these Hopes to ease my Grief,
Or bring to my despairing Soul Relief;
No, I'm too well acquainted with my Fate,
And know I'm born to be unfortunate.——

LETTERS OF A NUN

APPENDIX
Letter I

Yet while I write, some glimmering Hopes appear
That yield a respite to my wild Despair,
And some small Ease afford amidst my Care.
Tell me, what made you press my Ruin so?
Why with your Craft a harmless Maid undo?
Why strove t' ensnare my too-unguarded Heart,
When you were sure ere long you shou'd depart?
What Injury had I e'er done to you,
To make you with such Wiles, my Innocence pursue?

But pardon me, (thou Charmer of my Soul!)
For I will charge you with no crime at all.
Let me hear oft from you, where-e'er you are,
For I methinks shou'd in your Fortune share,
But above all, I beg you, by the Love
Which once you swore shou'd ever constant prove;
By all those Vows, which you so often made
When on my panting Bosom you have laid,
Let me no longer this sad Absence mourn,
But bless me, bless me with your kind Return.
Adieu—and yet so tender am I grown,
I know not how to end these Lines so soon;
Oh! that I could but in their Room convey
Myself, thou lovely faithless Man, to Thee!
Fool that I am, I quite distracted grow,
And talk of things impossible to do;
Adieu,—for I can say no more—Adieu.—
Love me for ever, and I'll bear my Fate,
(Hard as it is) without the least Regret.

LETTER II

From a Nun to a Cavalier

ALAS! it is impossible to tell
Th' afflicting Pains that injur'd
Lovers feel.
And if my Flame, by what I write,
you rate,
Then have I made my self unfor-
tunate.
Blest should I be, cou'd your own Breast define
The raging Passion that I feel in mine;
But I must ne'er enjoy that happy Fate:
And if I'm always doom'd to bear your Hate,
'Tis base to use me at this barb'rous rate.
Oh! it distracts my Soul when I reflect
Upon my slighted Charms, and your Neglect:
And 'twill t' your Honour as destructive be,
As 'tis conducive to my Misery.———

It now is come to pass what then I fear'd,
When you to leave me in such haste prepar'd.
Fool as I was, to think your Flame was true,
True as th' Excessive Love I bear to you!
T' encrease my Torments all your Acts incline;
To make me wretched is your whole Design.

APPENDIX
Letter II

Nor wou'd your Passion any Ease allow,
If only grounded on my Love for you :
But I'm so far ev'n from that poor Pretence,
Six Months are past since you departed hence;
Six tedious Melancholy Months are gone,
· And I've not been so much as thought upon :
Blind with the fondness of my own Desire,
Else might have found my Joys wou'd soon expire.
How cou'd I think that you'd contented be
To leave your Friends and Native Place for me ?
Alas ! Remembrance of my former Joys
Adds to the Number of my Miseries.
Will all my flatt'ring Hopes then prove in vain ?
Must I ne'er Live to see you here again ?
Why may not I once more behold your Charms,
Once more enfold you in my longing Arms ?
Why may not I, as heretofore, receive
Those sweet transporting Joys which none but you
   can give ?——

I find the Flame that set my Soul on Fire
In you was nothing but a loose Desire.
I should have reason'd ere it was too late,
And so prevented my approaching Fate :
My busie Thoughts were all on you bestow'd,
I for my own repose not one allow'd :
So pleas'd was I, whilst in your Lovely Arms,
I thought myself secure from future Harms :
But yet you may remember, oft I've said,
You'd be the Ruin of a harmless Maid ;
But those were Notions that abortive dy'd,
And I upon your flatt'ring Oaths rely'd.

PORTUGUESE NUN

Cou'd I cease loving you, I shou'd have Ease,   APPENDIX
But that's a Cure far worse than the Disease;   Letter II
And 'tis (alas) impossible, I find,
To raze your Image from my tortur'd Mind ;
And it's a thing which I did ne'er design,
For your Condition is far worse than mine;[1]
You'd better share what my poor soul endures,
Than th' empty Joys you find in new Amours.
So far am I from envying your Fate,
I rather pity your unhappy State.
I all your false dissembling Arts defie :
I know I'm rooted in your Memory,
And am perhaps the happiest of the Two,
In that I now am more employ'd than you.
They've made me Keeper of the Convent Door,
Which is a Place I ne'er supply'd before ;
It is an Office I ne'er thought t' have had ;
All who discourse me think that I am mad.
Our Convent too must be as mad as I,
Or they might have perceiv'd my Incapacity.

Oh ! how I wish to be as blest as they
Who, as your Servants, your Commands obey.
I shou'd be Proud, like one of them, to wait
On you, tho' 'twere ev'n in the meanest State.
My Love for you I don't at all repent ;
That you've seduced me, I am well content.
Your Rig'rous Absence, tho' 'twill fatal prove,
Yet lessens not the Vigour of my Love.
My Passion I to all the World proclaim,
And make no Secret of my raging Flame.

THE LETTERS OF A

APPENDIX Some Things I've done irregular, 'tis true,
Letter II And glory'd in them, 'cause they were for you;
My Fame, my Honour, and Religion, are
All made subservient to the Love I bear.

Whilst I am writing, I have no intent
That you shou'd Answer what I now have sent:
Force not your self, I'll not receive a Word
You send, that comes not of its own accord.
If not by writing you do Ease receive,
So't too to me shall Satisfaction give,
To Pardon all your Faults I'm much inclin'd,
And shall be pleas'd to prove you're not unkind.

I'm told that France has made a Peace; if so
A Visit here then sure you might bestow,
And take me with you wheresoe'er you go,
That must alone at your disposal be,
I fear (alas) it is too good for me.
Since you first left this sad forsaken Place,
I've not enjoy'd a Moment's Health or Ease:
The Accent of your Name my Cares abate,
Which I a thousand times a Day repeat.
Within our Convent some there are who know
From whence the Source of all my Sorrows flow,
Who strive to Ease me and Discourse of you.

I'm constant to my Chamber, which is dear
To me, because you've been so often there:
Your Picture as unvaluable I prize,
And have it always fixt before my Eyes:

PORTUGUESE NUN

The Counterfeit does Satisfaction give ; APPENDIX
But when I think that I must never live Letter II
To see the Bright, the Fair Original,
Great are the Horrors, great the Pains I feel,

Oh ! how I 'm wrack'd and torn with endless Pain
To think I ne'er must see you here again !
But why shou'd it be possible to be
That I your lovely Form no more must see ?
For ever ! are you then for ever gone ?
For ever must I make my fruitless Moan ?
No, Mariane, thou wilt soon have Peace ;
Kind Death approaches, he will give thee Ease.
Ah me ! how fast my fainting Spirits fail !—
Farewel, Oh, pity me !—Thou lovely Man,
Farewel.——

LETTER III

From a Nun to a Cavalier

HAT will become of miserable me?
What will th' Event of my Misfortunes be,
How can I hold, now all my hopes retire?
On them I liv'd, and must with them expire.
Where are the cordial Lines to heal my Pain,
T' assure me I shall see you here again?
Where are the Letters that should bring Relief,
Compose my Soul, and mitigate my Grief?

Fool'd with vain Projects, I of late design'd
To strive to calm and heal my tortur'd Mind :
The slender Hopes I have of seeing you,
Joyn'd with the Coldness of your last Adieu :
Th' Improbability of your Return,
The many tedious restless Nights I've born,
Your frivolous Excuses to be gone,
Encourag'd my Design and urg'd me on ;
Nor did I doubt Success till, ah ! too soon,
I found I still must love, still doat and be undone.

LETTERS OF A NUN

APPENDIX
Letter III

Wretch that I am! compel'd alone to bear
The heavy Burthen, which you ought to share.
You're the Offender, and I undergo
The Punishment, which ought to fall on you.
'Tis plain, I never yet enjoy'd your Love,
Since all my Torments can't your Pity move,
Feign'd were the Transports, false the Vows you made,
And only us'd that I might be betray'd.
Your whole Design was to ensnare my Heart
Then cruelly to act a Tyrant's Part.

T' abuse a Love like mine, is highly base,
And cannot but redound to your Disgrace.
Who would have thought, when of my love possest,
'Twas not enough to make you ever blest?
And 'tis for your own sake I'm troubled most,
When I but think upon the Joys you've lost:
Nay, did you judge aright,———
The difference soon by you perceiv'd would be,
Betwixt abusing and obliging me;
Betwixt the Pleasures, which you might have prov'd,
Of loving much, and being much belov'd.

Such is the Force of my excessive woe,
I'm quite insensible of what I do;
Ten Thousand different Thoughts distract my Mind,
My rigid Fate can't be by words defin'd;
To Death I love, yet cannot wish that you
Should share the Miseries I undergo.
To loath, t' have all things odious in your sight,
Receive no Ease by Day, no Rest by Night:

APPENDIX Your Soul o'erloaded with continual Cares,
Letter III Your Eyes still flowing with a flood of Tears;
Did you but suffer this my grief for you,
'Twou'd quickly finish what my own can't do.

Why do I write? Shou'd I your Pity move,
What good wou'd Pity do without your Love?
I scorn it; and my self with equal Scorn
I loath, when I reflect on what I've born:
My Friends I've lost, and Reputation too,
Have ran the hazard of our Laws for you:
But what's much worse, now I all this have done,
False as you are, ev'n you're ingrateful grown.

Yet, oh! I cannot, cannot yet repent,
But rather am with all my Ills content:
I cannot grieve at what I've done for you,
But more for your dear sake wou'd undergo;
To you wou'd sacrifice my Life and Fame;
They're yours, which you (and only you) can claim.

In short, I'm vex'd with every thing I do;
Nor can I think I'm kindly us'd by you.
False as I am, why don't I die with Shame,
And so convince you of my raging Flame?
If I had lov'd so well as oft I've said,
Your Cruelty ere this had struck me dead.
No, all this while, 'tis you've deluded been,
And have the greatest Reason to complain.
How could I see you go, and yet survive,
    out of Hopes of your Return and Live?
I've wrong'd you; but I hope you will forgive.

PORTUGUESE NUN

Yet grant it not, treat me severely still,   APPENDIX
Tell me, that I've abus'd, and us'd you ill.   Letter III
Be harder still to please, encrease my Care.
And end my Sufferings with a sure Despair.
A Fate that's Tragical would doubtless be
The Way t'endear me to your Memory.
Perhaps too you'd be touch'd with such a Death,
When you reflect how I've resign'd my Breath.
To me I'm sure, 'twou'd welcome be indeed,
And far to be preferr'd before the Life I lead.——

Farewel, I wish your Eyes I'd never seen,
But ah! my Heart, now contradicts my Pen.
I find I'd rather live involv'd in Harms
Than once to wish I ne'er had known your Charms.
And since you think not fit to mend my State,
I'll cheerfully (tho' hard) embrace my Fate.
Adieu,—but Promise me when I am dead,
Some pitying Tears you'll o'er my Ashes shed.
At least, let my too-sad Example prove
The means to hinder any other Love.
'Twill yield some Ease, since I must lose your Charms,
That you'll not revel in another's Arms.
Neither can you be so inhumane sure
To make my Fate assist a new Amour.
I fear my Lines are troublesome to you;
But you'll forgive my foolery—adieu,
Ah me! methinks too often I repeat
The Story of my too unhappy Fate;
Yet let me pay the Thanks to you I owe
For all the Miseries I undergo.

LETTERS OF A NUN

APPENDIX I hate the State in which I liv'd before
Letter III The more my Cares encrease, I'm pleas'd the more;
My Flame does greater every moment grow—
And I have still—Ten Thousand Thousand
Things to say to you.——

LETTER IV

From a Nun to a Cavalier

YE Gods! the Torments that from Love arise
When the dear Object's absent from our Eyes!
I'm told you've been by raging Tempests toss'd,
And forc'd to seek some Hospitable Coast,
The Sea, that is the faithless Lover's Foe,
I doubt will hardly e'er agree with you.
And oh! my Fears for th' Dangers you may meet,
Make me my own Tormenting Pains forget.

But is your Friend then more concern'd to know
Than I, the Perils that you undergo?
If not, how comes it that you cou'd afford
To write to him, whilst I have not a Word?——

Why do I talk? what cou'd I else expect?
But base Ingratitude, and cold Neglect?
From one who slighting all which once he swore
Now seeks new Beauties on a Foreign Shore.——
Yet Heav'n avert its Wrath, nor may'st thou be
E'er punished for thy Treachery to me,

THE LETTERS OF A

APPENDIX
Letter IV

For faithless as you are, I'm still inclin'd
Not to revenge, but rather to be kind.——

Tis plain, I'm now the least of all your Care,
Else you'd have some regard to My Despair.
But I, tho' wrack'd and torn with endless Pain,
To one relentless as the grave complain.
Yet I, fond I! regardless of my Fame,
Still Cherish, and Indulge this fatal Flame;
In vain my Reason offers to perswade,
I scorn its Counsel, and contemn its Aid,
And find a Pleasure in my being mad.
Had you but with this Coldness been possest,
When first you rais'd those Tumults in my Breast:
How many plagues had it from me detain'd!
How calm! how easie had I now remain'd!

But where's the Woman wou'd not have believ'd
Your Arts, and not have been (like me) deceiv'd?
Who cou'd your num'rous Oaths and Vows mistrust?
Who cou'd have thought that you shou'd prove unjust?
The frequent Protestations that you made
Wou'd have a Heart more firm than mine betray'd.
'Tis hard to think the Man whom once we love,
Shou'd false, shou'd cruel, and ingrateful prove.
Nay, I'm so easie, I've already made
Excuses for you, and wou'd fain perswade
My too too cred'lous Heart, that I am not betray'd.
It was your Converse that at first refin'd
My Ignorance, and till then, unpolish'd Mind.

PORTUGUESE NUN

APPENDIX
Letter IV

'Twas from your Passion that I caught this Flame
That is destructive to my Ease and Fame.
In vain 'gainst you I strove my Heart to arm,
For you in ev'ry Action had a Charm.
Your pleasing Humour, and the Oaths you swore,
Made me believe you ever wou'd adore.
But now (alas!) those grateful Thoughts are fled,
And all my Hopes are with my Pleasures dead:
I sigh and weep, a thousand Plagues possess
My Soul, and give me not a moment's Ease.
Great were my past Delights, I must confess,
Excessive were the Joys, and vast the Bliss,
But then, oh, cruel Fate! my Miseries were not
   less.——
Had I with Artifice e'er drawn you on,
And what I most desir'd have seem'd to shun;
Had I the cunning Arts of Women us'd,
And with feign'd Scorn your gen'rous Love abus'd;
Had I my growing Flame with Care supprest
When first I felt it rising in my Breast;
Nay, when I found I lov'd, had I conceal'd
My Passion, nor to you my Soul reveal'd,
That for your Hate had been some small Pretence,
Which you might now have urg'd in your defence;
But——
So far was I from using such Deceit,
My Heart was never conscious of a Cheat:
And I no sooner of your Passion knew,
But frankly I return'd the like to you.——

Yet you, tho' I was fondly blind, cou'd see,
Not ign'rant what the Consequence wou'd be.

THE LETTERS OF A

APPENDIX
Letter IV

Why with such Wiles then did you draw me on,
To leave me wretched, hopeless, and undone?
You knew you shou'd not long continue here,
And so did make me love but to despair.
Why was I singl'd out alone to be
Th' unhappy Object of your Cruelty?——
Sure in this Country you might those have met
Who were for your cross Purposes more fit;
Such, who by frequent Use had got the Pow'r
To give their Hearts but for the present Hour;
Who of your Falshood never wou'd complain,
Nor give themselves for you a moment's Pain.
Is't like a Lover then to use me so,
Me, who'd give up all I have for you?
Is it not rather like a Tyrant done,
To ruine and destroy what is your own?

Had you but lov'd so truly as you said,
You never from me in such haste had fled.
But you! how easie did you go away!
Nay, e'en seem'd pleas'd you cou'd no longer stay
The few Excuses that you made to go,
How slight they were! but any thing wou'd do,
To fly from one already nauseous grown,
That lov'd you but too well, and trusted you too soon.——

'My Friends (you cry) and Honour call me hence,
'And I must now be gone, to serve my Prince,'
Why was not that nice Honour thought on then,
When you deluded me to give up mine?

PORTUGUESE NUN

This was all Fiction, which you did devise   APPENDIX
To seem less guilty, and to blind my Eyes.   Letter IV
But, ah! should I have too much Bliss enjoy'd,
Might I with you have liv'd, with you have dy'd.——
My only Comfort is, I've been to you,
Spite of this Absence, constant, just, and true;
And can you then, who all my Thoughts controul,
And know the earnest Secrets of my Soul,
Can you be so regardless of my Pray'r,
T'abandon me for ever to Despair?
You see I'm mad, but yet I'll not complain,
For I'm so us'd to suffer your Disdain,
That now I find a Pleasure in my Pain.——

But what's my greatest Curse, those things no more
Can please me now, which I have lik'd before.
My Friends, Relations, and my Convent too,
Are odious all, and all detested grow,
Nay, ev'ry thing that not relates to you.
The flitting Hours of each succeeding Day,
If not on you bestow'd, I think they're thrown
   away.——

So great's my Love, and with such pow'r does rule,
It takes up the whole Business of my Soul.
Why then t'expel this Passion shou'd I strive?
For 'tis impossible I shou'd survive
This restless state, and with Indiff'rence live.

So much I now am chang'd from what I was,
That all observe and wonder what's the Cause:
My Mother chides, and urges me to tell
What 'tis creates my Grief, and what I ail,

THE LETTERS OF A

APPENDIX
Letter IV

I hardly know what Answers I have made,
But I believe that I have all betray'd.
The most severe and hardest Hearts relent,
And are with Pity touch'd at my Complaint.
To cruel Thee alone I sigh in vain,
For all the World beside compassionates my Pain.

'Tis seldom that you write, and when you do,
Your Lukewarmness each Line does plainly shew.
'Tis all but Repetition and Constraint,
Dull is each Word, and each Expression faint.——

My kind Companion took me t'other day
To the Balcon' that looks tow'rds Mertola;
The Sight so struck my Heart that, while I stood,
Strait from my Eyes a briny Deluge flow'd.
I then return'd, and strove to ease my Care,
For all my Thoughts brought nothing but Despair.
What others do to help me in my Grief,
Adds only to my Pains, and brings me no Relief.——

From that Balcon' I often took delight
To see you pass, and languish'd for the Sight.
'Twas there that fatal Day I chanc'd to be
When first my Heart resign'd its Liberty :
'Twas there I drew the Poison from your Eyes,
'Twas there this raging Passion had its rise.
Methought on me alone you seem'd to gaze,
And careless look'd on every other Face;
And when you stopt, I fondly thought to me
'Twas meant that I your lovely Shape might see.

PORTUGUESE NUN

I call to mind what Trembling seiz'd my Breast,   APPENDIX
Caus'd by a Leap given by your prancing Beast.   Letter IV
I near concern'd in all your Actions was,
Flatter'd my self I was of some the cause.
What follow'd, to relate I'll now forbear,
Lest you appear more cruel than you are;
And 'twill perhaps your Vanity encrease
To find my Labours have no more Success.
Fool as I am! to think to move you more
By Threats than all my Love cou'd do before!
Too well (alas!) I know my Fate to come,
And you're too too unjust to make me doubt my
    Doom.

Since I am not allow'd your Love to share,
All ills in Nature I have cause to fear.
I shou'd be pleas'd did all our Sex admire
Your Charms, if you did not return the Fire;
But there's no fear, I by Experience know
None ever long will be ador'd by you.
You'll easily enough forget my Charms
Without the taking others to your Arms.
By Heav'ns, I love, I doat to that degree,
That since I find you're ever lost to me,
I wish you 'ad some Excuse to hide your Crime,
That to the World you might less guilty seem.
'Tis true, 'twould make my Case but so much worse,
But then 'twould advantageous be to yours.——

While you are free, in France, perhaps the fear
Of not returning Love for Love may keep you there.

THE LETTERS OF A

APPENDIX
Letter IV

But mind not that, if you I sometimes see,
I shall contented with my Fortune be,
To know one country holds my Love and me.

Why with vain Hopes do I my Reason blind?
To one less doting you may prove more kind.
Pride in another may a Conquest gain
Greater than mine, with all the endless Pain
Of constant Love, which I've endur'd for you:
But, oh! from me take Warning what you do;
Retract your Heart ere yet (it) is too late,
And think upon my too too wretched Fate,
Reflect upon my endless Miseries,
Despairs, Distractions, and my Jealousies;
Think on the Trust that I've repos'd in you,
Th' Extravagance which all my Letters shew.

I well remember you in Earnest said,
For one in France you once a Passion had.
If she's the Reason why you don't return,
Be free, and let me thus no longer mourn;
For if my Hopes and Wishes are but vain,
Tell me the Truth——
And end at once my wretched Life and Pain.——
To me her Picture and her Letters send,
They'll make me worse, or else my Fate amend;
Such is the State of miserable me,
That any change would advantageous be
Your Brother's and your Sister's send me too,
All will be dear to me that's so to you.——

PORTUGUESE NUN

APPENDIX
Letter IV

Methinks I cou'd submit to wait upon
The happy Woman that your Heart has won,
So humble am I made by all your Scorn,
And the ill Usage that from you I've born ;
Scarce dare I say, I may myself allow
To Jealous be, without displeasing you,
Fain wou'd I think that I mistaken am,
And fain perswaded be, that you ar not to blame.

The Person that's to bear these Lines to you,
Wants to be gone, and does impatient grow.
I thought in this not to have giv'n Offence,
But yet I'm fall'n into Extravagance.
And now methinks 'tis time that I had done,
But I've no Pow'r to end these Lines so soon,
Nor force the pleasing Vision from my Sight ;
My lovely Charmer's present while I write.
Twelve solitary Months are almost past
Since in your trembling Arms you held me last,
And fondly, to my Ruin, me embrac'd.
Fierce, and true as mine, I thought your Flame,
And, oh ! believ'd 'twould always be the same.
Ne'er cou'd I think, that when you had enjoy'd
My Favours, with them you'd so soon be cloy'd :
Or that the Dangers of the Sea you'd run,
Scorn Rocks and Pirates too, that you might shun
A Maid that lov'd like me, and is by you undone.
Reflect, thou faithless Man ! and call to mind
What I've endur'd for you, yet not repin'd,
And tell me, can this Treatment then be kind?

LETTERS OF A NUN

APPENDIX
Letter IV

The Officer now presses me to 've done
My Letter, or (he says) he must be gone;
He's as impatient, as if he, like you,
Were running from another Mistress too,
Farewel—from me you parted with more ease
(Perhaps for ever too) than I can do with these.

My Mind a thousand pleasing Notions frames,
And I cou'd call you many tender Names;
More dear than is my Life to me, are you;
And dearer far than I imagine too;
Sure never any yet so cruel prov'd,
To be so barb'rous when so well belov'd.

'Tis hard to end,—See I begin anew,
And th' Officer won't stay; oh! let him go:
I write to entertain my self, not you;
And 'tis so long, you'll never read it thro',
Gods! how have I deserv'd such Plagues as these?
And why was you pick'd out to spoil my Peace?
Oh! why was I not born where I might pass
In Innocence and Happiness my Days?
'Tis too too much to bear, no Tongue can tell
What I endure—Farewel—false Man!—Farewel,
See! see! how miserable I'm made by you,
When I dare not so much as ask your Love—adieu.

LETTER V

From a Nun to a Cavalier

HOPE, by th' different Ayre of this,
    you 'll find
That as I 've chang'd my Stile, I 've
    chang'd my Mind.
The Substance of these Lines will
    let you know
That you 're to take them for my last Adieu:
For since your Love is past redemption gone,
I 've no Pretence to justifie my own.
All that I have of yours shall be convey'd
To you, without so much as mention made
Of your loath'd Name; the Pacquet shall not bear
Those Letters which I now detest to hear.

In Donna Brites I can well confide,
And whom, you know, I 've other ways imploy'd;
Your Picture she 'll (and all that 's yours) remove,
Those once-endearing Pledges of your Love:
A thousand Times I 've had a strong Desire
To tear and throw them in the flaming Fire;
But I 'm a Fool too easie in my Pain,
And such a generous Rage can't entertain.

APPENDIX Wou'd but the Story of my Cares create
Letter V The like to you, methinks 'twou'd mine abate.
Your Trifles, I must own, went near my Heart,
With them I found it difficult to part.
To what was yours I bore such mortal Love,
Tho' you yourself did quite indiff'rent prove,
They've cost me many a Sigh, and many a Tear,
And more Distraction than you e'er shall hear.
My Friend, I say, now keeps them in her Pow'r,
And I am never to behold 'em more;
She them will secretly to you convey,
Without my Knowledge hasten them away:
Tho' for a sight I on my Knees shou'd lie,
The more I pray, she must the more deny.

Ne'er had I known the Fury of my Flame
Had I not try'd my Passion to reclaim;
Nay, to attempt a Cure I'd ne'er begun,
Cou'd I've foreseen the Hazards I must run:
For sure I am, I cou'd with greater Ease
Support your Scorn, as rig'rous as it is,
Rather than to retain the dreadful Thought,
That Absence must for ever be my Lot.

I shou'd be happy if I cou'd be Proud,
And with the Nature of our Sex endow'd:
Cou'd I despise you, and your Actions scorn,
And be reveng'd for all the Ills I've born.

Fool as I am, to let my hopes rely
On one who strives t'encrease my Misery!
You talk of Truth and Sincerity;
They both are what you never shew'd to me.

PORTUGUESE NUN

To tell you what I've born 'tis now too late,   APPENDIX
(For th' most obliged, and yet the most ingrate)   Letter V
Let it suffice I all your Falsehood know;
And all I ask for what I've done for you,
Is, Write no more, but some Invention find
To tear your Image from my Tortur'd Mind.

I too must now forbear to write to you,
Lest a Relapse shou'd by that means ensue;
And the Event of this I've no Desire to know.
Methinks you shou'd enough contented be
With th' Ills you have already brought on me:
Sure now you need no more molest my Ease,
Or shake the Structure of my future Peace.
Do you but leave me in Uncertainty,
I hope in time I shall at quiet be:
'Tis not impossible but I may find
A Love as true as you have been unkind.
But what will Love that any Man shall shew
Afford to me, without I love him too?
Why shou'd his Am'rous Passion more incline
To move my Heart, than yours was mov'd by mine?
And I perceive by what I now endure,
That the first Wounds of Love admits no Cure;
All sorts of Remedies then prove in vain,
W' are ne'er recover'd to our selves again;
So fixt, and so immutable is Fate,
We're doomed to Love, though w' are repaid with Hate.

I'm sure I cou'd not so hard-hearted be,
To treat another as you've treated me:

THE LETTERS OF A

APPENDIX Provided you was to another chang'd,
Letter V Of you I cou'd not that way take revenge.
I'd fain perswade my self a Nun shou'd ne'er
Confine the Passions of a Cavalier;
But if a man wou'd by his Reason move,
A Mistress in a Convent is most fit for Love;
Those in the World do all their Thoughts employ
On Balls, on Visits, and their Finery,
Encrease their Husbands' Jealousies and Cares,
Whilst those who favour us have no such Fears.
' Alas! we've nothing here to change Desire,
But by Reflection daily fan the Fire.

I wou'd not have you think that I maintain
These Arguments, in hopes I may regain
Your Love; too well I know my Destiny;
I always was, and still must wretched be.
When you was here I did no Rest enjoy:
Present, for fear of infidelity;
When distant, Absence did my ease destroy.
I always trembled while you was with me,
Lest you shou'd be found, and come to Injury:
While in the Field, both Lives in Danger were;
Fear of my parents did encrease my Care.
So that 'tis plain, ev'n at the best, my Mind
Was as disturb'd as I at present find:
Since you left me, had you but once seem'd kind,
I shou'd have follow'd, and not been confin'd.
Alas! what wou'd have then become of me,
T' have brought a Scandal on my Family;
T' have lost my Parents and my Honour too,
And, after all, to be despis'd by you?

PORTUGUESE NUN

APPENDIX
Letter V

What Thoughts soever you of me retain,
I reconjure you ne'er to write again :
Methinks you shou'd sometimes reflect upon
The base ungen'rous Injuries you 've done.

No woman sure did e'er so easy prove ;
What did you ever do to gain my Love?
You was the first that to the Army went ;
To stay the longest there, the best content.
Did you more careful of your Person grow,
Altho' upon my knees I begg'd you wou'd do so?
Did you e'er strive to fix in Portugal,
A Place where you was well belov'd of all?
Your Brother's Letter hurry'd you away,
On the receipt of it you 'd not a moment stay ;
And I 'm inform'd you ne'er was pleased more
Than when on board a making from our Shore.
You can't deny but you deserve my Hate,
And I may thank my self for all my Fate ;
I was too free, and gave my Heart too soon,
And brought upon my self the Ills I 've undergone.
Alas ! from Love alone Love ne'er will rise,
It must be rais'd by Skill and Artifice.
Your first Design was to ensnare my Love,
And nothing wou'd have spar'd that might successful
    prove :
Nay, I believe, if it had needful been,
Rather than failed, you wou'd have lov'd again ;
But you found easier ways to work upon,
And thought it best to let the Love alone.——

Perfidious Man ! which way can you atone
For th' base and treach'rous Affronts you 've done?

THE LETTERS OF A

APPENDIX
Letter V

The blinding Passion now is vanquished quite,
That kept the foulness of them from my sight:
Must my tormented Soul never have Ease?
When shall I be, thou cruel Man, at Peace?

Within a while you yet perhaps may hear,
Or have a Letter, from your injur'd Fair,
To let you know that she is at repose,
Freed of the Torments that from you arose.
Oh! what a Pleasure it will be to me,
Without concern t' accuse you of your Treachery!
When I've forgot the wracking Pains I've born,
And able am to talk of you with Scorn!

You've had the better, it is plainly prov'd,
Because I you have out of Reason lov'd;
But by the Conquest you small Honour won,
For I was young, and easily undone.
I, whilst a Child, was cloister'd, knew no hurt,
Discours'd with none but of the vulgar Sort,
And what belonged to Flatt'ry never knew,
Till I unhappily was taught by you:
You'd a good Character of every one,
Which you made use of to entice me on.

My Indignation, and your Falsehood too,
Makes me at present much disorder'd grow;
But, I assure you, I will shortly find
Some Means or other for to ease my Mind.
Perhaps may take a way to quit my Care
Which, when 'tis acted, you'll be pleas'd to hear.

PORTUGUESE NUN　　　　　　　APPENDIX
　　　　　　　　　　　　　　　　　　　　Letter V

Fool as I am, to say thus o'er and o'er
The same that I 've so often said before !
Of you a Thought I must not entertain,
And fancy too I ne'er shall write again ?
For what occasion 's there that I to you
Shou'd be accountable for all I do ?

THE END OF THE NUN'S LETTERS.

Edinburgh: T. and A. CONSTABLE
Printers to Her Majesty

www.ingramcontent.com/pod-product-compliance
Lightning Source LLC
Chambersburg PA
CBHW031826230426

43669CB00009B/1237